Dawn of Victory

BREAKTHROUGH AT PETERSBURG
MARCH 25-APRIL 2, 1865

by Edward S. Alexander

EMERGING CIVIL WAR SERIES

Chris Mackowski, series editor
Daniel T. Davis, chief historian

Also part of the Emerging Civil War Series:

Dawn of Victory

BREAKTHROUGH AT PETERSBURG
MARCH 25-APRIL 2, 1865

by Edward S. Alexander

EMERGING CIVIL WAR SERIES

SB

Savas Beatie
California

First edition, first printing

ISBN-13: 978-1-61121-280-8

Library of Congress Control Number: 2015932291

Published by
Savas Beatie LLC
989 Governor Drive, Suite 102
El Dorado Hills, California 95762
Phone: 916-941-6896
Email: sales@savasbeatie.com
Web: www.savasbeatie.com

Savas Beatie titles are available at special discounts for bulk purchases in the United States by corporations, institutions, and other organizations. For more details, please contact Special Sales, P.O. Box 4527, El Dorado Hills, CA 95762, or you may e-mail us as at sales@savasbeatie.com, or visit our website at www.savasbeatie.com for additional information.

To Chris Mackowski,
whose guiding hand brought this book to life

Table of Contents

Union generals hoped their men would not get bogged down under artillery fire while negotiating the tangled lines of abatis in front of the Confederate works. (hw)

*Footnotes for this volume are available at
http://emergingcivilwar.com/publications/the-emerging-civil-war-series/footnotes*

List of Maps

Maps by Hal Jespersen

Acknowledgments

I would like to first and foremost thank my parents, Steve and Jane Alexander, who always showed great support along the way in my goal to become a park ranger and historian. My heartfelt appreciation also goes to Alison Foster who provided unyielding emotional support while patiently understanding the late research nights and unexciting weekends during the writing process.

Snow covers a battery at the Hart farm. (ea)

Great thanks to Chris Mackowski and Dan Davis, who served as content editors for the book. Without Chris's remarkable inspiration and faith in me, this project would have never left the ground. I am forever grateful for his belief in me and encouragement at every step along the way. I also greatly appreciate Dan's energy in putting together a nice appendix piece that covers action elsewhere in Virginia, allowing me to concentrate my time on Petersburg. It is also a great pleasure and privilege to work with the entire group at Emerging Civil War, who daily cranks out exciting new pieces about a century-and-a-half old event.

I would like to thank Theodore Savas and the staff at Savas Beatie, whose great care in helping a new guy learn the ropes made this entire process enjoyable. My appreciation also goes to Hal Jespersen of cwmaps.com for providing excellent maps of the campaign. I also offer a big-shout out to Ryan Montgomery for the incredible aerial photographs of the battlefield.

This being my first published book, there are a few individuals who deserve acknowledgement for forging me in the past into the historian I am today. Thanks to Greg Mertz and Jake Struhelka, who pushed me to form my own "interpretive voice." I am also grateful to John Hennessy at Fredericksburg and Spotsylvania National Military Park for providing my first real opportunity in 2010 to practice the craft of primary source research.

To A. Wilson Greene and Patrick Olienyk at Pamplin Historical Park, thanks for standing by me through my first trying years as a brash young park ranger. I especially appreciate Will's blessing to tackle a project he had previously mastered with his seminal book, *The Final Battles of the Petersburg Campaign.*

The Fortification Exhibit at Pamplin Historical Park offers a unique look inside the earthworks. (ea)

Great contributions to the remembrance of this story were also made by Chris Banchero and Bill Heinrich, fellow rangers at Pamplin Historical Park. Together we have tramped most of the ground covered by this book, building more trails and restoring more historical viewsheds than you would ever think a three-man department could accomplish.

I'd also like to thank Jeb White at Station 2 in Richmond, whose patient and flexible scheduling assisted me in funding and accomplishing this project. And I certainly will never forget the memorable group of staff and regulars there who became my extended family here in Virginia. Particular thanks to Sean Caldwell, who relentlessly called me out to actually get out there and turn my book dreams into a reality.

PHOTO CREDITS:
Edward Alexander (ea); Auburn University (au); Castletown Foundation (cf); Daniel T. Davis (dd); Edwin Forbes: *An Artist's Story of the Great War* (ef); *Frank Leslie's Illustrated Newspaper* (fl); *Harper's Weekly* (hw); Library of Congress (loc); Library of Virginia (lv); National Archives (na); Pamplin Historical Park (php); Ryan Montgomery (rm); Petersburg National Battlefield (pnb); U.S. Army Military History Institute (usmhi); University of Virginia (uva); Virginia Historical Society (va.hs); Vermont Historical Society (vt.hs); White House Historical Association (whha)

For the Emerging Civil War Series

Theodore P. Savas, *publisher*
Chris Mackowski, *series editor*
Daniel T. Davis, *chief historian*
Sarah Keeney, *editorial consultant*
Kristopher D. White, *emeritus editor and co-founder*

Maps by Hal Jespersen
Design and layout by Chris Mackowski

"The turn of things on that memorable morning
was a turn that filled the soul with gladness.
At dawning of day, we could see comrades bleeding,
dying and dead, and it was sad to see our fallen heroes,
but high above the sobs of death could be heard the shouts
of victory, victory, victory."

— *Sgt. Francis Cordrey*
126th Ohio Infantry

Prologue

APRIL 1, 1865

The heavens raged on the night of April 1, 1865, as Union artillery, ringing the embattled city of Petersburg, unleashed a thunderous rain of shot and shell. One hundred and fifty guns pelted the Confederate fortifications with the "arrows of a fiery archer." Like an unending earthquake, the constant rumble shook the soldiers who hugged the damp ground to their core.

Lieutenant General Ulysses S. Grant hoped the bombardment could soften up the Southern defenses for his army's pending front assault but, despite its tremendous show, the vicious barrage caused little material damage.

A Union soldier who witnessed the numerous explosions over the earthworks believed his opponents must have regarded this thundering and lightning as the "vengeful wrath" of Uncle Sam that signaled their "impending doom." Despite those confident assertions, another officer realized the grave implications for this deafening cannonade: "The shriek of the shot and shell gave us an idea of what we might expect in the morning."

For nearly three hours the bombardment continued, muffling the tramp of 14,000 Federal infantrymen who jostled into position to attack just before dawn. "Before the light of another day, we shall charge the rebel works, all are talking about it; all dread it," confided a worried New Yorker. As a Pennsylvania regiment reached their jumping-off point, a private confessed, "If we have to charge these works, I will never get alive over."

Though they still could not see their objective, each soldier knew what lay ahead. Together they had formed "a living wedge to penetrate the strongest line of works ever constructed in America."

Confederate artillery position on the Breakthrough Trail at Pamplin Historical Park (ea)

"It would seem that the devils in hell were fighting in the air," recalled a Connecticut captain. (php)

In their front waited massive mounds of dirt piled to afford generous shelter from the cannonade for their defenders. The Federal soldiers expected the lines bristled with small arms and artillery of its own.

Beyond the walls, a simple plank road wound its way through the Dinwiddie County countryside, paralleled as it entered Petersburg by the only railroad still servicing the city from the south. The vital transportation hub at Petersburg lay just 20 miles below the fledgling rebellion's capital of Richmond.

OPPOSITE: Union artillery batteries on Petersburg National Battlefield's western front. (rm)

On to Richmond!

CHAPTER ONE

Richmond, Virginia, had always been the focal point during the American Civil War. "On to Richmond!" guided the Union Army of the Potomac in all their travels. The home population begged for it, the press screamed for it, the politicians promised it, and the soldiers hummed its namesake tune on the march. The capital of the Confederacy mockingly stood just 100 miles south of Washington, D.C. Most assumed the capture of this city would symbolize that secession had failed, believing that, as the Stars and Stripes marched triumphantly down its streets, the other rebelling states were sure to rejoin the Union.

But Richmond proved to be a hard road to travel.

McDowell at Manassas, McClellan on the Peninsula, Pope yet again at Manassas, Burnside at Fredericksburg, Hooker at Chancellorsville. Each stopped prematurely in the tracks of their "On to Richmond" quest; each disgracefully joining the list of castoff generals who failed to deliver. After taking command of the Confederate Army of Northern Virginia in June 1862, Gen. Robert E. Lee repeatedly demonstrated an ability to read his opponent during the campaign and bring the battle to them on his own terms.

Initially, many of Lee's soldiers reacted disgustedly to his appointment, calling him "Granny Lee" or the "King of Spades" due to his penchant for digging in while McClellan's massive army slowly lumbered toward the Confederate capital. Their appetite for the offensive was soon fulfilled, however, when they realized that Lee viewed his army's large earthen fortifications as a springboard for the vicious attacks he unleashed upon his numerically superior foe. That summer, he drove the

Only the center portion of the Virginia State Capitol stood in 1861. The building also served as the Capitol of the Confederacy. (ea)

LEFT: **Despite failing health and a weakened army, Robert E. Lee still presented a wily adversary to the Union generals.** (loc)
CENTER: **President Lincoln instructed Ulysses S. Grant: "Hold on with a bulldog grip, and chew and choke as much as possible."** (loc)
RIGHT: **George Gordon Meade struggled as Union commander, with his boss, Grant, always looking over his shoulder.** (loc)

Union away from the capital, previewing his strategy the next time the Northern army threatened the city so closely.

After a year of mostly unchecked victories, save for a harrowing near-disaster along Antietam Creek near Sharpsburg, Maryland, Lee had the ultimate confidence in his men, and they now shared that assessment of their commander. In the summer of 1863, he again took the destructive fighting outside of Virginia, this time advancing all the way into Pennsylvania before facing a more determined foe enjoying the material, morale, and logistic advantages of fighting on their native Northern soil.

After three days of intense fighting around the small hamlet of Gettysburg, Maj. Gen. George G. Meade at last boasted an unquestionable combat victory over Lee. Despite this battlefield victory, President Abraham Lincoln felt disappointment at Meade's sluggishness in following up success and his inability to destroy Lee's army before they safely returned to Virginia. After a hastily aborted Union offensive that November again failed to produce decisive results, the commander in chief realized he must again seek yet another leader to guide Union forces to their ultimate goal.

Lincoln's gaze turned to the star of the West— the architect of victories that year at Vicksburg and Chattanooga—Ulysses S. Grant. The Union army's performance in the western theater under Grant's command far outpaced their eastern counterparts, but he had never faced an adversary matching the quality of Lee or the Army of Northern Virginia. Grant's success did not rest on his tactical brilliance on the battlefield but instead on an understanding of the logistics necessary to support a prolonged campaign and the endurance and innovation necessary to see it to its end. He effectively besieged the Mississippi River citadel at Vicksburg to open the entire course of the vital lifeline, then relieved the stranded Union elements at Chattanooga—feeding and supplying the troops before military action brought final control of Tennessee. These merits brought Grant east into command of all Union forces.

Upon his arrival in March 1864, Grant intended to have the various Union armies spread throughout the South finally act in concert with one another. In his official report for the final campaign, he wrote:

> From an early period in the rebellion I had been impressed with the idea that active and continuous operations of all the troops that could be brought into the field, regardless of season and weather, were necessary to a speedy termination of the war. . . . The armies in the East and West acted independently and without concert, like a balky team, no two ever pulling together, enabling the enemy to use to great advantage his interior lines of communication for transporting troops from east to west, re-enforcing the army most vigorously pressed, and to furlough large numbers, during seasons of inactivity on our part, to go to their homes and do the work of producing for the support of their armies.

In the fourth year of the war, President Abraham Lincoln also had to focus on his campaign for reelection. (loc)

Abraham Lincoln agreed with Grant's determination for all the Union armies to act as one and used a far simpler description: "Those not skinning can hold a leg." Grant detailed orders for five Union armies to carve up the Confederacy. While smaller forces threatened Richmond, the Shenandoah Valley, and Mobile, Alabama, Grant's former command out west, now under Maj. Gen. William T. Sherman, would move on Atlanta. With Gen. Joseph E. Johnston's Army of Tennessee under constant pressure, the Union plan prevented them from reinforcing vulnerable targets.

Grant kept Meade in command of the Army of the Potomac, camped near Culpeper, and instructed him to focus less on Richmond and more on its defenders. "Lee's army will be your objective point," he instructed the 48-year-old Pennsylvanian. "Wherever Lee's army goes, you will also go." Grant also intended to follow wherever Meade went, placing his headquarters in the field with the Army of the Potomac.

That route first took them into the Wilderness, near the previous year's battlefield at Chancellorsville. Grant hoped to compel Lee's force out of their defensive positions constructed along the Rapidan River. He believed Meade's men could crush their opponent once it was drawn into the open. Lee struck the Union army as they moved through the Wilderness, and fighting raged on May 5-6 that produced heavy casualties but few strategic gains.

The Capitol building stands out in this view of wartime Richmond. (loc)

Rather than retreat and regroup after a large battle as his predecessors did, Grant ordered Meade to move past Lee's right flank and speed for the open ground and roadways around Spotsylvania Court House. The Confederates won the race and established field fortifications northwest of the county seat. For two weeks, the Union army tried to break this line until, once more, turning Lee's flank and continuing their movement to the southeast.

Lee's smaller force outpaced their counterparts and quickly dug in along the North Anna River. The wily Confederate commander hoped to ensnare Grant's army as it negotiated a crossing but fell sick before he could spring the trap. Recognizing the danger, Grant withdrew and, instead, continued his maneuvering to the southeast, soon approaching McClellan's old battlefield near the capital.

Reaching the Cold Harbor crossroads at the start of June, the Union general in chief wanted to continue to press on for Richmond. Exhaustion in the ranks from their month-long campaign and a fracturing relationship between himself and Meade hampered Grant's plans, resulting in a poorly executed attack on June 3.

Grant recognized the Cold Harbor line was untenable and decided to make the unpopular decision to turn his sights away from Richmond. His plan all along had been to destroy Lee's army, but they remained as formidable an opponent as ever in the desperate defense of their capital. But with the Confederates pressed into their earthworks around Richmond, their supply lines stood vulnerable for the taking.

On June 12 the Union army secretly abandoned their field fortifications around Cold Harbor and swiftly marched for the James River. Crossing on transports and a remarkably built pontoon bridge over the wide-spanning

Union engineers constructed a 2,100 foot pontoon bridge over the James River near President John Tyler's former estate. (loc)

tidal river, Grant hoped to capture the transportation hub before Lee could react.

Colonel Edward Porter Alexander, a Confederate artilleryman, gave Grant all the credit for the conception and execution of the movement: "The orders & details of such a rapid movement of so mighty an army, with all its immense trains & its artillery, across two rivers, on its own pontoon bridges, make it also the most brilliant piece of logistics of the war." He had a lesser assessment of his army, who he complained "had lost Grant and was sucking its thumbs by the roadside 25 miles away, and wondering where he could be."

As two corps of the Union army marched toward Petersburg from City Point—the confluence of the James and Appomattox Rivers—only 2,200 Confederates awaited in the city's defenses.

Petersburg Besieged
CHAPTER TWO

Despite the city's strategic value, the Union army did not threaten Petersburg until 1864. While the Army of the Potomac fought its way through central Virginia in May, Grant instructed Maj. Gen. Benjamin Butler's Army of the James to move up the Bermuda Hundred peninsula to cut the Richmond & Petersburg Railroad. Butler's campaign stalled, and a small Confederate force bottled up his army on the peninsula.

Butler tried once more to directly capture Petersburg while the Army of the Potomac floundered around Cold Harbor. He instructed a force of nearly 5,000 infantry and cavalry to cross the Appomattox River and invest the city on June 9. The infantry aimed for the eastern defenses of the town before balking at the enemy fortifications. Meanwhile, Brig. Gen. August V. Kautz's cavalry swept for the Jerusalem Plank Road to the south.

The Federal troopers ran into the 125-man battalion of Virginia Reserves, a motley unit consisting of Petersburg's old men and young boys. The militia delayed Kautz long enough for additional reinforcements to rush to Petersburg's inner lines, compelling the Union to abandon the expedition.

Infused with great devotion to the defense of Petersburg, Brig. Gen. Henry A. Wise, former Virginia governor and now commander of the city's garrison, declared on June 12: "Petersburg is to be and shall be defended on her outer walls, on her inner lines, at her corporation bounds, on every street, and around every temple of God and altar of man, in her every heart, until the blood of that heart is spilt. Roused by this spirit to this pitch of resolution, we will fight the enemy at every step, and Petersburg is safe."

The largest fortification around Petersburg, Fort Fisher contained nineteen artillery positions. (ea)

Henry Alexander Wise served as Virginia governor from 1856-1860. (loc)

That same day, unknown to Wise, the Union army began their withdrawal from the Cold Harbor line, with Petersburg in their sights.

*   *   *

In 1860, Petersburg's population numbered 18,266, including 3,164 free blacks and 5,680 slaves. It ranked as the second-largest city in Virginia and seventh-largest in the Confederacy. The city's location at the fall line of the Appomattox River made it the primary market for many farmers in southern Virginia and North Carolina. An elaborate rail system connected the city to Richmond, Norfolk, City Point, Lynchburg, and North Carolina. Fearing that their sellers might bypass their market, city officials refused to allow each of the five railroads that entered Petersburg to connect with one another. The Confederate government eventually forced a throughway due to military necessity.

Petersburg rapidly grew during the boom in the decades preceding the war as the fertile ground now being planted west of the tidewater regions produced high crop yields. From the constant flood of goods into the city's tobacco warehouses and cotton mills, the city extravagantly improved its infrastructure, featuring cobblestone and granite streets lined by brick sidewalks and gaslights. In 1856, the city established a municipal water system with two large reservoirs on the southeastern outskirts.

Petersburg, Virginia, has still not recovered its prewar prosperity, ruined by the nearly ten-month grip of both armies. (loc)

The city enjoyed a proud military legacy dating back to a spirited resistance by Virginia militia against the British army on April 25, 1781. During the War of 1812, the Petersburg Volunteers served effectively in the northwest under William Henry Harrison. Local tradition claims that President James Madison reviewed this company on their return home and dubbed Petersburg the "Cockade City of the Union" in reference to the prominent insignia on their caps. The nickname grew in popularity in the two decades before the American Civil War, forever stamping the city of Petersburg with its mark.

While Kautz's June 9 battle with the militia signaled the first combat around the city, Confederate officials had previously taken great measures to provide for its protection. When McClellan threatened the region in 1862, authorities contracted Capt. Charles H. Dimmock to construct a 10-mile line of defenses around Petersburg. Soldiers and slaves built 55 artillery batteries, each in mutual support of its neighbors and connected by rifle

The Cockade City was once picturesque and bustling. (hw)

pits. These ready-made defenses proved vital to Robert E. Lee, who had lost track of Grant's movements north of the James.

*   *   *

Major Generals Winfield S. Hancock and William F. Smith led the II and XVIII Corps from City Point to the Dimmock Line on June 15. Only a token force stood in their way of capturing the city. Both deferred from ordering a committed attack, however, buying time for Lee to transfer reinforcements. Over the next few days both sides funneled more troops to the eastern side of Petersburg. By June 18, the Union army advanced in force but ran into a well-entrenched foe. Grant quickly realized he could not take the city by frontal assault:

"Lee's whole army has now arrived, and the topography of the country about Petersburg has been well taken advantage of by the enemy in the location of strong works. I will make no more assaults on that portion of the line, but will give the men a rest, and then look to extension toward our left, with a strong view of destroying Lee's communications on the south and confining him to a close siege."

For more than nine months he attempted to capture Petersburg. Though the Union army never completely surrounded the city to qualify as the true definition of a siege, the massive earthworks constructed by both sides often led the soldiers to consider themselves as participants in that stagnant form of warfare. In reality, however, the campaign for control of the Cockade City relied far more on maneuver than the sprawling fortifications suggested.

Recognizing that direct assault against the Confederate earthworks would produce only unnecessary bloodshed with no strategic gain, Grant targeted the supply lines. In late June, he seized the Jerusalem Plank Road before temporarily halting his efforts on Petersburg

Though the Petersburg campaign never truly met the definition of a siege, this period of the war is most famous for the elaborate fortifications constructed by both armies. (loc)

to dispatch the VI Corps to Washington to stop a Confederate raid on the Union capital. He also needed time for his army to refit from their strenuous campaign across Virginia and consolidate after the loss of many three-year volunteer units who joined up in the summer of 1861.

By 1864, both armies needed little motivation to dig in at their current location for safety. (hw)

With the strategic situation beginning to bog down, Grant authorized a daring plan devised from within the ranks of the IX Corps to counter the nuisance of the ever-present Confederate earthworks. A group of coal miners tunneled underneath the enemy line with the idea of setting off a mine that, upon explosion, would form a large gap in the fortifications to create space for infantry to rush forward and capture Petersburg. To deflect attention from this operation, Grant transferred the II Corps back across the James River to threaten Richmond and draw Lee's focus from Petersburg.

The ruse worked to perfection. While six Confederate divisions hustled to the defense of the capital, only three remained behind in Petersburg on July 30—the morning of the explosion. However, poor leadership in the IX Corps doomed the tragic action that became known as the battle of the Crater.

Despite this setback, Grant learned that the pressing necessity of protecting the Confederate capital handcuffed Lee to Richmond. In later offensives, the Federals always threatened north of the James before making major strides against a

severely reduced foe, thus allowing Federals to make gains along the road network south of Petersburg. In late August, for instance, Union columns once more marched on Richmond before returning back to seize the tracks of the vital Weldon Railroad.

The Union army strengthened their control of the Weldon Railroad with the construction of large earthworks like Fort Wadsworth. (fl)

In just over two months of combat since reaching Petersburg, Union successes reduced the city's defenders to two supply lines running southwest—the Boydton Plank Road and South Side Railroad. Grant attempted to capture these routes in late September, but after his forces ran into fierce fighting around Peebles Farm, he advised his generals not to try the main Confederate earthworks that extended along the plank road.

Though Grant minimized his losses in killed and wounded in these offensives and gained ground in each step along the way, the prolonged campaign to capture Petersburg received harsh criticism from the Northern public. He attempted once more to cut the city off in late October, but after the II Corps barely fought their way back from a trap set for them south of Hatcher's Run, the Union general in chief decided not to risk any more losses before the presidential election.

By keeping the bulk of Lee's army confined to Virginia through the year, Grant set up his other subordinates for success. General Sherman captured Atlanta on September 2 and soon unleashed a destructive war against the Southern economy and will to fight in his famed "March to the Sea." On October 19, Maj. Gen. Philip H. Sheridan defeated Lt. Gen. Jubal A. Early at Cedar Creek to gain control of the Shenandoah Valley.

Portions of Fort Wadsworth's parapets still stand today. (ea)

The next month, Sheridan relinquished the VI Corps back to the Army of the Potomac. Once more, the wearers of the Greek Cross set off for Petersburg.

Winter Quarters

CHAPTER THREE

Major General Horatio G. Wright's VI Corps arrived back in Petersburg in early December and settled in south of the city. They found a drastically different strategic situation than the one they had left in early July. Second Lieutenant George Oscar French used the grave of his friend killed in June near the Jerusalem Plank Road to track the Union army's progress during their absence: "When we left, this spot was two miles in front & beyond our left, now Grant's left is some six miles to the front. I tell you Grant has done well here." He was relieved to report: "The grave was all right except we found a railing around it & a better headboard than we had been able to furnish for him."

Mementos from the violent battles around Petersburg frequently reminded the VI Corps soldiers of the terrible carnage. "The government are lifting all the Union dead and burying them all in a cemetery a little bit in rear of our camp," chronicled a Pennsylvanian in early January. With cold weather reducing the frequency of combat, the soldiers turned their attention to the struggle for comfort as they settled into position between the Jerusalem Plank Road and where the Union line fish-hooked opposite Tudor Hall.

"The winter was passed in hard picket and fatigue duty," remembered a Vermont soldier who frequently found himself close enough to the enemy pickets to spend his shift talking back and forth with his counterparts. The increasing scarcity of wood often caused these adversaries to bond together to reduce their suffering. One day the Vermonter met a Confederate between the lines and together they cut down a tree, "he chopping

Built just before the war, the Hart house served as William MacRae's headquarters during the winter encampment at Petersburg. (ea)

one side and I the other." After it fell, they divided the log and returned back to their respective camps.

The close proximity between the armies piqued the curiosity of all who visited that winter. A Northern newspaper publisher traveled to Petersburg curious to see the now-famous city. He called on an old friend, Col. Erastus D. Holt of the 49th New York, and together they rode near the picket line. Noticing his companion

The Sixth Corps placed their winter quarters on the previous summer's battlefield – "Rather a hard place for nervous and superstitious men." (fl)

straining for a better view, the colonel pointed to a tall pine near the front line and said, "Mack, by climbing that you can get a sight of Petersburg."

The newspaperman thought it would be a sight well worth seeing and climbed the tree to enjoy the view before the colonel noticed the Confederate pickets nearby acting strange and called out that he might soon get a few shots taken at him. The civilian returned to the ground on his own, deciding he "had rather climb down than fall down; for the fall might hurt some."

The constant labor of Union engineers soon produced a better means of spying on the enemy than the few remaining trees in the dwindling Dinwiddie County forests. The 50th New York Engineers began their construction on December 20 of a 14-story signal tower with a 40x40 foot base. They built the observatory from nearby timber that they secured with screws, bolts, and braces. "This is a very disagreeable task to be done at this season when cold winds are so frequent," commented one of the Yankees, but he nevertheless expected to overlook the entire Confederate left and the various roads leading in and out of Petersburg. "By means of the tower, we shall be kept informed of all movements of troops on the part of the enemy."

A Union officer with a good view of Petersburg reported that the two armies seemed "so close to each other and so peaceful in appearance." (hw)

The Southerners tried to harass the construction by occasionally firing on it to no avail. Severe weather more seriously delayed the completion of the project, but the engineers finished by late February. On St. Patrick's Day, which was marked by great festivities in the camps of the II Corps, Capt. Charles C. Morey of the 2nd Vermont found opportunity to visit the tower and look over the Union and Confederate camps. Upon reaching the top he could finally see over the Confederate earthworks to the object of their protection, claiming he "could see the cars on the Southside Railroad."

Many Confederates also took special interest in the tower. "From its top the curious Federals have the satisfaction of seeing all that is going on in our lines," wrote a Maryland soldier. "They will next mount a telescope to ascertain what we eat and the color of our hair. Go ahead, Mr. Yankee! But use it for religious purposes, as the top of your observatory is the nearest you will ever get to heaven." If the Union soldiers had scrutinized the Confederate winter camps closely they would have discovered a life of haves and have-nots.

Union engineers constructed this signal tower near their fish-hook line around Forts Fisher and Welch. (php)

*   *   *

Following the battle of Peebles Farm, Brig. Gen. Samuel McGowan placed the headquarters for his five South Carolina regiments at the vacated home of Joseph G. Boisseau on Duncan Road. His men hurriedly threw up earthworks in early October to protect Petersburg's two remaining supply lines while his staff settled in to their new home and office.

"It was very pleasant at brigade headquarters at the Boisseau house," commented Lt. James Fitz-James Caldwell, who stayed upstairs in the plantation home. "We had visits from General Heth, General Wilcox, General MacRae and others of that rank, and had frequent visits from officers of the brigade. General McGowan was a hearty, genial, entertaining host."

The lieutenant spent the winter months writing the military history of the brigade and found ample opportunity to remain cultured as he passed the time: "In the absence of books, we frequently entertained one another with recitals from the poets and dramatists. General McGowan led in this, having committed to memory many passages of Milton, Shakespeare and others."

Major General Cadmus M. Wilcox established his division headquarters at Cottage Farm on Petersburg's outskirts. The Tennessee native commanded McGowan's South Carolinians as well as Brig. Gen. Edward L. Thomas's Georgians and Brig. Gens. Alfred M. Scales and James H. Lane's two North Carolina brigades.

The 50th New York Engineers also constructed an elaborate gothic church out of pine logs at the site of what is now Poplar Grove National Cemetery. (loc)

Major General Henry Heth, a fellow Third Corps division commander, settled near Tudor Hall at the Pickrell house. He procured a blockade runner at Wilmington to import luxury items to send by wagon to Petersburg loaded with coffee, ham, brandy, and tea. Lieutenant Colonel Walter H. Taylor, Lee's adjutant,

A modest plantation home for the Boisseau family for fifty years, Tudor Hall would witness one of the most decisive battles of the war. (rm)

wrote fondly on November 27 about the beautiful horse Heth received from Wilmington, "to say nothing of the fine cigars, nice white sugar, good whiskey (a secret), etc to all of which we did full justice."

Heth's four brigades—Joseph R. Davis's Mississippians, William McComb's Tennesseans, and John R. Cooke and William MacRae's North Carolinians—continued the Boydton Plank Road fortifications toward Hatcher's Run.

Meanwhile General Lee relocated his headquarters that month to the western outskirts of Petersburg. Taylor chose the Turnbull house, Edge Hill, for the general to stay in. "Here I am finely fixed in the parlour with piano, sofas, lounges, pictures, rocking chair, etc." commented the adjutant, "everything as fine as possible for a winter campaign."

Back around Tudor Hall, officers jockeyed for precious furloughs home or arranged for their wives to join them at the front. "Are you making preparations to come out here this winter?" wrote South Carolina surgeon Spencer G. Welch to his wife. "A great many other officers are arranging for their wives to come on soon. Some of them are here already." Upon arrival, Mrs. Welch found her stay to be most comfortable, though she could not help but notice some of the disparities between the officers and enlisted men: "Over here we have good wood in abundance, and keep roaring fires all the time. I wish our soldiers on the line were as fortunate. Wood is scarce there and then only green pine, for which they have to go some distance into the country."

* * *

While McGowan's staff recited Shakespeare from their warm quarters at the Boisseau house, their troops enjoyed a considerably less comfortable stay. One of the brigade sharpshooters described his winter hut: "The foundation for each shanty was made by digging into the face of the hill and drawing the earth back on the lower side. Chimneys were cut into the wall on the deepest side of the excavation. The lower side was built up to a level with small timbers and a fly tent stretched over the whole."

A South Carolina politician and lawyer by trade, Samuel McGowan was commended for gallantry for his service in the Mexican War. (php)

A North Carolinian down the line, no doubt by this point in the war used to cramped quarters, sarcastically provided blueprints for his shared space: "I think by Tuesday evening the Capt. and I will get into our shanty, it will be a small room, only 9 by 11 feet, for kitchen, bedroom, parlor and dining room, but then I think we can make it comfortable for the winter."

Unable to rely on the crumpling Confederate infrastructure, many Southern soldiers improvised their meals however they could. "The other day I got tired of bacon and corn bread and determined to have some good soup," wrote a member of McGowan's Brigade. After filling up a pan with rice and water, he fried some bacon and added the meat and grease to his concoction, thickening it with his leftover corn bread. Gathering some red pepper and onion, he seasoned the mixture and let it simmer. "The soup turned out to be rather thick," he recalled, "but of the very best quality and good enough for anybody."

But even those basic staples sometimes proved difficult to find. "Our rations consisted of one pound of corn meal and a third a pound of bacon per day and we thought the weight was light at that and the commissary did not have bacon to issue all the time," complained another South Carolinian.

Throughout their struggle, many in the Confederate army still clung to the belief that Robert E. Lee could still deliver the victories on the battlefield that defined his first year in the Army of Northern Virginia. "The fate of the Confederacy rested alone upon the shoulders of this incomparable leader; to whom all looked, both soldiers and citizens, for deliverance," declared one of McGowan's officers. "Times look gloomy to my eyes," wrote a North Carolinian," but hope this gloomy shadow will be taken away soon."

The soldiers found what entertainment they could. When not chopping wood or foraging and fishing for additional supplies, the Confederates also enjoyed music, playing practical jokes, skating on a frozen Hatcher's Run,

and paying visits to Petersburg or to friends in nearby units. Yet these distractions could not replace the longing desire by many in both armies to finally return to their loved ones. Many unable to secure a furlough faithfully wrote home at every moment.

"I pray God I may be spared to see the end of this 'cruel war' and return home to your side to live a peaceful

"All Winter the Rebels have been working like beavers, strengthening and perfecting their works. . . . As far as can be seen are heavy lines of breastworks, and connected forts so spaced and located as to cover each other, and in case of an assault, sweep their whole front with a cross fire . . . that would annihilate anything on legs." (ef)

and happy life," wrote a North Carolina lieutenant to his sweetheart. "Money and property I do not crave for now, it is peace, one that will give us peace now and durable— an honorable peace one for which I have been marching, suffering, fighting and bleeding for these three years and a half."

During the winter, an opportunity arose to bring a peaceful resolution to the conflict that gripped the nation the previous four years. On February 3, President Lincoln and Secretary of State William H. Seward met with three Confederate commissioners, including Vice President Alexander H. Stephens, aboard the steamer *River Queen* to discuss terms for peace. The Southern delegates left the meeting frustrated by Lincoln's steadfastness that national reunification was a prerequisite to ending the war.

When McGowan's Brigade learned of the conference and were told of President Lincoln's terms, they held a vote for determination on the question of submission. "The poll was taken," recalled a South Carolinian, "an every mother's son of them voted to fight it out to the bitter end."

The topic of arming of the slaves briefly came up in the Confederate army. "I suppose that they are going to put in the negroes in the army. I think that will not do, for the white soldiers they say that they won't stay here," guessed Cpl. Benjamin H. Freeman. Upon later reading that the Confederate Congress passed an act on March 13, 1865, authorizing the recruitment of black soldiers, the North Carolinian wrote, "I hope they will not send them to the army for I don't want to fight with the negroes."

The officers of the 49th Georgia, however, favored this proposition and passed around a resolution declaring:

Soldiers entertained themselves as best they could on the front lines but had to be ever mindful of the harassing sharpshooters' fire. (hw)

"We did not consider it disgraceful to labor with negroes in the same field, or at the same work bench, we certainly will not look upon it in any other light at this time, when an end so glorious as our independence is to be achieved."

While the addition of black soldiers into the ranks would relieve pressure off the rapidly diminishing Confederate armies, many took a strong position similar to a sergeant who declared, "I did not volunteer my services to fight for a free negroes free country, but to fight for a free white man's free country & I do not think I love my country well enough to fight with black soldiers."

The North Carolinian could not stomach the implications that military service entailed. "If they are put in the army they will be on the same footing with the white soldiers, will receive the same rations, the same clothing & the same pay that the white soldier gets & as it is pointedly against the wills of nearly all the soldiers they will not submit to such wrongs & there is but one way they can escape such wrongs & that is to desert which they are doing every night."

Desertion proved to be a major problem for the Confederate army, especially after Grant released his Special Orders Number 3 in January. The order promised that if any Confederates delivered themselves to the Union lines, they would not be treated as prisoners if they took an oath stating they would not take up arms against the United States. Instead they would receive food and transportation to any location held by Federal forces. Grant also offered deserters a chance to gain employment in a non-combat role in the army and hoped to coax more over by providing rewards for any weapons, horses, or equipment brought in by the Confederates.

"There was seven of our men from the Brigade run off last night from the line," wrote Corporal Freeman. "I expect that all will run off before long." Some did not mind the loss of the irresolute deserters. "The chaff was winnowed from the wheat," believed a North Carolinian. Major Harry Hammond of McGowan's Brigade agreed, writing, "I do not think the desertions have weakened us of materially and I trust that it may prove to have added morally to us by relieving us of the disaffected."

Occasionally, however, the entire picket line or whole companies would desert in one night, creating irreplaceable losses in Lee's thinning army. "They have to place three videttes," joked a New Jerseyman, "one to watch us, the one in the rear to watch him, and still another to watch them both."

Increasingly, Confederate soldiers not native to Virginia lost interest in Ulysses S. Grant's army at Petersburg and focused their concern on Sherman's army ravaging their way through Georgia and the Carolinas. Letters from the home front did little to encourage the troops to remain in the trenches. Major Hammond recounted the grief of a fellow staff officer who learned that stragglers from Sherman's march stayed at his home for seven days "and destroyed everything." The officer's wife wrote that she had to huddle in the parlor with her young two children the entire time.

Advanced picket posts allowed forward observation points and served as early warning in case of an attack. (loc)

Eventually, the Union pickets expected each night for a handful to cross over, and they were happy to let Lee's army bleed away without a large battle. A New Yorker claimed, "If we had been content to remain long enough, we might have received them all without the firing of a gun."

The Northern pickets also found humor in coaxing deserters over. "Hello, Yank, have you got any coffee?" called out a Confederate one night. "Plenty, have ye got any Johnny cake?" was the response in return. "Plenty," replied the Confederate who hoped to sweeten the deal by adding, "& plenty of butter." The Yankee laughed back. "Well, then, grease your backsides & slide into the Union."

These earthworks on Petersburg's eastern front show the landscape's sudden transformation into military use. (loc)

Trading indeed was common between the pickets. "It was a very simple process," explained a member of McGowan's Brigade. "A Yankee out on the picket line would shake a paper or bundle of coffee and holler at us as to what he had to exchange with us and he would place it on a stump or some elevated place, and go off;

then we would go and get it and leave our package for the party to come for. I never knew or heard of either party cheating."

Private Perry's experience on the picket line suggested otherwise. He chronicled in his diary on March 16 that the sent an unarmed man halfway across the lines after an agreement to trade with the Confederates. When the Union soldier drew close to the Southern lines, the Confederates opened fire. "We quickly flew to our rifle pits to protect our man. . . . Then our men begun to call the Rebels liars fools and traitors . . . we laid low and kept Johnny Reb in his hole. We all had to be careful after this incident."

The clichéd tales of tobacco-for-coffee trading between the lines is a common component in veterans' recollections of Petersburg. (ef)

* * *

Both sides frequently used the informality of the picket line to assist with gathering intelligence. Major Thomas J. Wooten of the 18th North Carolina established a daring reputation for his raids, boasted by his comrades as a "terror to the enemy's picket lines." During the day, Wooten feverishly scouted the Union rifle pits for a soft spot. Once darkness fell, he positioned a deep two-row column to dash all the way through the designated spot on the line with as little noise as possible. Wooten led from the front but always halted at the rifle pits as his storming party dashed through. Once the last two Confederates passed Wooten, he ordered both ranks to face outward and wheel back on the unsuspecting Federal pickets from the rear, gobbling up captives.

These frequent expeditions kept rookies to the picket line constantly spooked. "Twenty times during my hour of duty my musket was cocked, and by stooping I was almost certain that the rebs were upon us, as I could see them, in imagination, approaching," confessed a Vermont private. "But the hour passed—after two or three weeks, as it seemed to me—and no rebs appeared."

Colonel Thomas W. Hyde was frustrated one night by awaking to a dozen bullets ripping through the canvas roof of his hut after another Confederate raid. He requested permission to stage one on his own. Before Meade gave his authorization, though, Confederates took advantage of the fraternity between the pickets on the eastern side of Petersburg to stage one of their most desperate assaults of the war.

Jones Farm

CHAPTER FOUR

By March of 1865, Robert E. Lee once more had a crisis on his hands. Many in his army had lost the will to fight and longed to return home after four years of indecisive combat. Despite having fewer soldiers to feed and equip, the unreliable Southern infrastructure prevented Lee's veterans from receiving adequate supplies to keep pace with Grant's men. Even if the Confederates around Richmond and Petersburg could hold off the Union armies in their front, Lee increasingly worried about Sherman's eventual arrival from the Carolinas. Together, Grant and Sherman would present an unbeatable combined foe.

The Union general, meanwhile, wanted to act as soon as possible, but two considerations delayed his campaign. The repetitive freeze-thaw cycle compounded by heavy rains during the early months of 1865 left the road network around Petersburg muddy and impassable for the Union artillery and wagon trains. Grant needed to wait for the roads to sufficiently dry to continue expanding his logistical monster around the Cockade City. While he did not anticipate for Sherman to start his movement from North Carolina until April 18, he eagerly expected the return of his cavalry, which was currently mopping up the remains of Jubal Early's army in the Shenandoah Valley. On March 2, Maj. Gen. Philip H. Sheridan defeated the Army of the Valley at Waynesboro and would soon return to the Army of the Potomac.

Lee, knowing he had to take urgent action before that reunion, hoped to once more take the initiative and bring the next battle closer to his own terms.

*   *   *

These rifle pits at the Jones Farm are unique in their appearance. Originally built by the Confederates, Union soldiers repurposed them to face the other direction after their capture. (ea)

Union control of the Weldon Railroad at Fort Wadsworth prevented a direct connection south for Lee. (fl)

The weary chieftain called his youngest corps commander, Maj. Gen. John B. Gordon of the Second Corps, to his headquarters on March 4 and detailed the remaining options for the Confederacy:

> *First, make terms with the enemy, the best we can get. Second, if that is not practicable, the best thing to do is to retreat—abandon Richmond and Petersburg, unite by rapid marches with General Johnston in North Carolina, and strike Sherman before Grant can join him; or, lastly we must fight, and without delay.*

Earlier attempts at finding a peaceful end to the war that would guarantee Southern independence had failed, but Lee once more proposed to meet with his opponent in early March to discuss these possibilities. Grant forwarded that message on to his commander in chief. President Lincoln responded to "hold no conference with Lee except for the surrender of his army."

With the likelihood of being able to sue for an agreeable peace continuing to decline, Lee turned his hopes to the rendezvous with Johnston in North Carolina, finally leaving behind the tightening noose within the Richmond and Petersburg defenses. This proved to be a near insurmountable challenge. Lee had to orderly withdraw his army from nearly 40 miles of entrenchments and race to the west so that he could turn the corner south into North Carolina ahead of Grant.

Despite having no previous military training or experience, John Brown Gordon proved to be an effective commander during the war. (loc)

Recognizing that difficulty, the Confederate commander chose instead call once more on the aggressive spirit of his Army of Northern Virginia.

With all other possibilities exhausted, Gordon realized his superior had already made up his mind. "To stand still was death," the corps commander agreed. Lee tasked Gordon to find the ideal location on the front to rupture the enemy lines; Gordon scouted the Union earthworks until he found a suitable target: Fort Stedman.

Here the two sides were only 200 yards apart from

one another. Just 50 yards separated the pickets. Gordon hoped to noiselessly capture the Union sentries by sending in men posing as deserters. He detailed three hand-picked storming parties to move on Fort Stedman and its neighboring batteries.

The Second Corps commander believed that the capture of this fort and its secondary line would open up the military railroad at Meade's Station to a raid that would follow Lee's strategy. If the Confederates severed the bulk of Grant's men from their supplies, Lee could force the Union army to constrict their lines and consolidate closer to City Point. With some much-needed breathing room gained, the Confederate army could make their direct move south into North Carolina to continue the war.

The Union generals relied on the combined strength of their fortifications and artillery, more than massed infantry, to defend Petersburg's eastern front. (ef)

Recognizing that this bold maneuver offered the only chance of escaping from Richmond before Sheridan and Sherman's arrival, Gordon discussed an unconventional plan with his subordinates. "I can take their front line any morning before breakfast," declared one of Gordon's division commanders.

While getting to Fort Stedman should prove easy, Gordon needed sufficient force to stay there.

Lee authorized Gordon to strip the western front lines thin by transferring two brigades from Lt. Gen. Richard H. Anderson's Corps and four brigades from Lt. Gen. A. P. Hill's Third Corps to bolster his attack. The Georgian still felt that he could use more men and received Lee's permission the day before the battle to bring Maj. Gen. George Pickett's Division south from Richmond. On paper, Gordon now had half the infantry in the Confederate army available for his offensive.

However, Pickett did not arrive on time to participate, and Hill's men did not receive specific instructions for their role in the battle. Nevertheless, the Third Corps men abandoned their sections along the main line guarding the Boydton Plank Road west of Petersburg and marched to the other side of the city, though they never received orders putting them into combat. The Confederate brigades left behind in Dinwiddie County spread their ranks even thinner and prayed Union scouts would not notice the mass exodus to the east.

Gordon detailed pioneers to remove the obstacles in front of Fort Stedman to guarantee its capture. (hw)

Gordon's assault proved successful to the point of capturing Fort Stedman, but the Confederates failed to expand their breech to the north and south. More Second Corps men poured into the maze of trenches behind the fort to the east but failed to reach the railroad at Meade's Station. Meanwhile, Maj. Gen. John G.

Parke, commanding the Federal IX Corps, rallied reinforcements to the scene.

The attack cost between 2,500-3,000 of Lee's best men and did not achieve any significant changes to the strategic picture on the eastern front. By the evening, the consequences of its failure would doom the Confederate line west of Petersburg.

To his credit, General Meade reached an appropriate conclusion from the near disaster at Fort Stedman. He addressed the battle in his General Orders Number 13 that sought to reclaim the initiative and set the stage for the coming Union campaign:

President Lincoln supposedly pointed at Confederate prisoners from Fort Stedman and declared: "Ah, there is the best dispatch you can show me from General Parke." (hp)

Two lessons can be learned from these operations: One, that no fortified line, however strong, will protect an army from an intrepid and audacious enemy, unless vigilantly guarded; the other, that no disaster or misfortune is irreparable where energy and bravery are displayed in the determination to recover what is lost and to promptly assume the offensive.

*   *   *

Private William Perry's sleep was rudely interrupted at 4 o'clock by the sound of gunfire to the east. Convinced that trouble was brewing, he quickly shook his drummer awake and advised him to beat the long roll. The musician listened for just a few moments before agreeing that "Hell is to pay up there."

In a flash, the camps along the VI Corps line bustled with energy as companies hurriedly rushed to the breastworks expecting the Confederates to appear in their front. After a New York private reached his post, he found that he had put his pants on backwards in his haste. "But I had my cartridge-box on and my musket loaded, ready for the fray."

John Grubb Parke took command of the IX Corps following Burnside's failure at the Crater. (loc)

As the excitement died down, the men stacked their arms and cooked breakfast. Soon, a courier rode up and reenergized the camp with news that the Confederates had captured Fort Stedman and were moving on the railroad to destroy the army's supply line. General Wright lent Brig. Gen. Frank Wheaton's division to Parke to help stabilize the situation on the eastern front. By the time this command reached Stedman's vicinity, they found "old glory was waving over it and our services for the time were not required."

Despite Wheaton's departure, the VI Corps commander aggressively remained focused on the enemy in his front. He believed the Confederates must have weakened their lines to provide the offensive firepower at Fort Stedman. With communications with Meade not back up, he turned to Parke for guidance: "As the enemy have massed on the right of our line they must have left their own line weak. How would it do for us to attack along the whole length of our line?"

As he awaited authorization, though, Wright began doubting his offensive. He asked to scrub the operation once contact with Meade was reestablished.

Meanwhile, on the left of the VI Corps, Maj. Gen. Andrew A. Humphreys came to a similar impression about the weakened lines along the Boydton Plank Road and drove in the Confederate pickets that fronted his II Corps near the Watkins house. Inspired by news of this success, Meade instructed Wright to test the pickets in front of Fort Fisher.

The VI Corps commander reluctantly turned to his Third Division to probe the enemy position. Brigadier General Truman Seymour already had the 14th New Jersey out on picket in front of Fort Fisher and the 10th Vermont in front of Fort Welch. He reinforced these units with the 122nd and 110th Ohio, respectively. Lieutenant Colonel George B. Damon of the 10th Vermont took command of the expedition, which lay in a mile long front 300 yards from the Confederate rifle pits. Around 1 p.m. he signaled their advance.

Horatio Gouverneur Wright took over leadership of the VI Corps after the death of their beloved commander, John Sedgwick, on May 9, 1864 at Spotsylvania. (na)

"Away we went across a flat through one swamp," wrote a corporal, "the Johnny's rifles cracking like corn in a hot skillet, the bullets whirring around us every jump." Damon claimed his own regiment breached the picket line but their support gave way. The combined fire from the rifle pits and the Confederate main line forced the Union skirmishers to retire back to their original position.

"My first attack on the enemy's picket-line has failed," Wright reported. "I shall try it again with troops enough for an assault, as soon as they can be got in position." Doubt still lingered, however, in the skeptical general's mind. "The enemy is strong in my front, and I think I may fail."

For the next two hours, Wright carefully crafted a plan of attack supported by heavy reserves. Colonel J. Warren Keifer took his men out of their fortifications around Fort Welch and placed them among the debris of Damon's battered command east of Arthur's Swamp on the left of the movement. To his right-rear, Col. James M. Warner took a support position between Forts Welch and Fisher. The Vermont Brigade prepared to charge in front of Fort Fisher. Brigadier General Lewis A. Grant massed his men in a heavy column. To their right, Col. Thomas W. Hyde stood in support with his brigade.

Finally a flag waved from Fort Fisher to signal the charge. "Forward they went on the run," recalled 1st Lt. Charles H. Anson, who admitted that many a heart

One of George B. Damon's soldiers wrote that on March 25 their officer "rode boldly along the line where not one of them was allowed to stand up, with a storm of bullets falling around him constantly." (vt.hs)

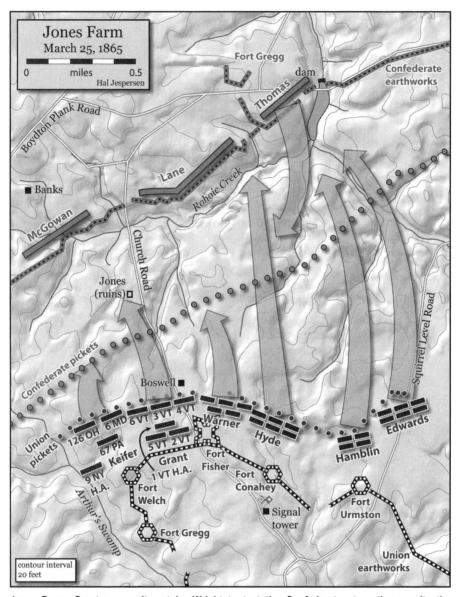

JONES FARM—Greater commitment by Wright to test the Confederate strength opposite the VI Corps lines on March 25 could have resulted in the capture of the weakened Confederate position. As it stood, the VI Corps's gains gave the April 2 assault its opportunity to succeed.

trembled "while facing that hail storm of shot and shell and musket ball."

In some spots, the Confederate skirmishers fought valiantly to slow the onslaught. "On they came, shoulder to shoulder, the stars and stripes flying over their heads," described Sgt. Berry Benson from the main line. "Our men, kneeling in the pits, take good aim and we can see how busy they are. It is but a minute before the enemy's

Construction of Fort Welch, named for a colonel killed at Peebles Farm, began in early October 1864. (ea)

line falters, appears about to break and flee. But look, the color bearer runs forward alone with his flag. With a shout that rings again, the blue line follows in a swift charge through our deadliest fire."

Benson may have seen Pvt. George H. Littlefield of the 1st Maine Veteran Volunteers. The regiment's flag bearer fell wounded while Hyde's men charged forward, and the private scooped up the colors and bore them to the front. For his conspicuous gallantry, his commander officially promoted Littlefield to color corporal on the following day. Three months later, he earned the lone Medal of Honor received by the VI Corps for its March 25 engagement.

Soon Hyde's men ran into the Rohoic Creek dam that immediately arrested their progress. The colonel sounded the recall, and the men fell back to align with Grant's brigade who found only token resistance along Church Road. "They only fired once and then threw down their guns," claimed a Vermonter.

After they gained the rifle pits, the men continued on past the Jones house. Some enthusiastic fellows continued the charge on McGowan's main line of fortifications before the assault spent its last energy and fell back. "The rebels do not fight as well as they did one year ago," observed Capt. Charles Morey. "We advanced to within 30 rods of their main line of works but were not strong enough to take them so we contented ourselves with what we had already gained."

Wright's men did not have long to rest on their laurels. Brigadier General Edward L. Thomas observed the withdrawal of McGowan's pickets from his entrenchments along Rohoic Creek. He summoned two of his regiments, the 45th and 49th Georgia, to attack across McIlwaine Hill to reclaim the position. Colonel Thomas J. Simmons took command of the pair. Confederate engineers had built a large dam across the

Sergeant Berry Benson had recently returned to the Confederate army after a daring escape from a northern prison. (php)

Colonel Augustus Wade Dwight's mother mourned the loss of her son: "Of our grief, I cannot and will not speak; it is the story of thousands of mothers and sisters all over our desolated land." (php)

An interpretive trail rings a small portion of the rifle pits still preserved at the Jones farm. (ea)

creek in Thomas's front, and the Union had veered away from this seemingly impassable pond in their assault. Their right flank now lay open for a swift response.

"As we passed the crest of the hill, we saw the baleful foe on forbidden ground," wrote Capt. John Hardeman of the 45th. "With a yell from one end our line to the other that made the welkin ring, we were up and at them. . . . Our line was good, our yell frightful, our fire murderous, and our victory complete." The Georgians threw the Union flank back in confusion, but not before Lt. Col. Charles A. Conn fell dead; his last words, "Forward boys, forward."

The appearance of the Georgians forced Colonel Hyde to deploy the 1st Maine Veterans and 122nd New York to the right to meet the threat. The regiment's reorientation to the east placed them squarely in an enfilading fire from the main Confederate line. A shell flew in and decapitated Col. Augustus W. Dwight of the 122nd. "I feel as though I had lost a father," mourned one of men.

The Georgians occupied the original rifle pits east of Church Road for more than an hour before Wright prepared another force to storm the position. Brigadier General George W. Getty's division marched forward once more at 5 p.m. "The hill was blue as far as we could see," wrote Captain Hardeman. "Our two regiments, numbering in all about four hundred guns, fought them

until they were within fifty yards." Colonel Simmons gave the order to retreat but some Confederate remained in the pit "and gave the Yankees the benefit of the butt of their guns." Meanwhile Col. Joseph E. Hamblin's brigade swung in from the right and trapped several hundred of the Georgians before they could make it back to their lines.

By nightfall, the VI Corps had reestablished their hold on the Confederate rifle pits. On March 26, they repurposed them to serve as their own picket post. "All day long we worked hard turning the works to face the other way, and by dark we were quite safely intrenched in our new and advanced line," recalled a New Yorker. "We could look right into the camps of the enemy."

The VI Corps charged across Joseph C. Boswell's farm along Church Road to reach the Confederate rifle pits. (php)

General Grant was ecstatic with the Union aggressiveness in the afternoon. He told Meade, "It reflects great credit on the army for the promptness with which it became the attacking force after repelling an unexpected attack from the enemy."

Yet as the Union soldiers settled back into their camps after their engagement, they were disgusted by the slight appreciation heralded to their efforts. Colonel Hyde particularly found offense with a newspaper that buried their combat at the bottom of an article on Fort Stedman: "There was heavy skirmishing on the lines of the 6th corps yesterday."

Their battle did, however, open up new remarkable opportunities.

Lieutenant Colonel Hazard Stevens, of Getty's staff, recognized the "incalculable advantage" of the ground now possessed by the VI Corps. "From it all the intervening ground to the enemy's main line could be closely scanned as well as his works themselves, and room was secured to form an attacking column in front of the Union works and within striking distance of the enemy's. One salient point of the new fortified line . . . commanded an excellent view up and down their main line for a considerable distance."

Stevens referred to McIlwaine Hill—a location of grave concern to the Confederate high command. From an elevated position on McIlwaine Hill, Union artillery could deliver a devastating crossfire onto part of the Confederate line.

William S. Dunlop wrote Lee's Sharpshooters in 1899 to detail the experience of these specialized battalions in the last year of the war. (php)

*   *   *

On March 26, Lee called Cadmus Wilcox to his headquarters. Wilcox's men would bear the brunt of any artillery barrage from McIlwaine Hill—so Lee ordered Wilcox to recapture the hill. Wilcox, in turn, designated the 400 men of his sharpshooter battalions for the assignment.

Major Thomas J. Wooten of Lane's Brigade and Capt. William S. Dunlop of McGowan's Brigade positioned their Carolinians on the front line with plans to storm the Federal line. Immediately they would wheel to the right and left to clear the way for the rest of the sharpshooters to storm up the hill through the newly forged opening.

This March 28 sketch made from Fort Fisher shows the barren ground between the two lines. (loc)

McGowan stressed the importance of McIlwaine Hill to his subordinate, claiming it "must be recovered from the enemy at all hazards."

Dunlop understood, remembering the sharpshooters stood "determined to take the hill or impale ourselves on the enemy's bayonets which bristled along the crest in solid mass."

As the small band quietly moved forward they found their advance stalled by a dry branch of Rohoic Creek. They encountered "a ditch, densely hedged on both sides with briars and thorns," when close to the Union line, but pressed forward, struggling to maintain their silence. "As we drew nearer the enemy, the snapping of sticks, the rustling of brush seemed to me so loud that I could not understand how we went so far undiscovered," worried a sergeant.

With the front lines only 30 paces from their objective, a picket finally fired out the alarm. The sharpshooters countered with a Rebel Yell and quickly rushed forward before the main Union line could react. "The fury of the struggle was but for a moment," claimed Dunlop. A Vermonter agreed, writing, "They boys was scared and run back."

While the daring attack prevented artillery use of McIlwaine Hill, Wilcox did not have enough manpower to also throw back the newly established Union rifle pits on the other side of Church Road. The two sides settled into their slightly rearranged positions and the pickets soon began to pop away at each other.

Inadvertently, both sides attempted to prank their counterpart in the same fashion. "We would put our caps upon our bayonets above the pit for the enemy's sharpshooter to fire at, and thus expose their positions," wrote a New York private, who noted that the Confederates soon filled the hat full of holes.

Meanwhile Sergeant Benson claimed that he advanced ahead of his own rifle pits with a handful of comrades, where they "tied a coat to a stick or ramrod, and placing a hat on it, poked it up cautiously." After the Union pickets opened fire they dropped the dummy and heard a great cheer from the Northern lines. "The trick was played for some time before they found it out. And even then we could sometimes fool them by moving the dummy along as though it were a man walking."

While the skirmishers had their fun, Federal scouts and officers quickly gathered intelligence on the main Confederate line from their close proximity along the advanced line.

On the night of March 28, Col. Oliver Edwards ordered his brigade pickets to advance as close to their Confederate counterparts as possible and listen in on their conversations. Private William W. Perry crawled to within 15 feet on his hands and knees and listened as the Carolinians spoke of home. "The northern army is too strong for us and I for one am tired," stated one of the Confederates who also claimed to regret ever going to war. Perry heard him state the he would happily surrender after fighting nearly four years with nothing to show for it. The other agreed and believed that Lee intended to soon evacuate Petersburg, but cautioned, "He had better soon be at it or he would never get out."

More important than listening in on the frustrated banter between pickets, the VI Corps officers also used their new advanced line to gain additional topographical knowledge of the Confederate earthworks.

Lieutenant Colonel Stevens described the terrain between the lines:

Edward Lloyd Thomas relied on the inundation from a military dam on Rohoic Creek to mask the small number of his Georgians. (php)

> *The ground here was nearly level, dropping off on the left into a shallow marshy hollow, which narrowed to a ravine next to their works, and extending on the right to the artificial ponds which here protected their line. Thick pine woods covered all this ground in the beginning of winter, but these had been cut down and removed for fuel by the troops of both sides, and many of the stumps had been cut even a second time close to the earth. . . . There was an opening besides, wide enough for a wagon to pass, which they used to send out for wood. The enemy had through a plank across the ditch at this point, not far from the ravine, and the Vermonters watched his pickets crossing on it and passing through the abatis as they went out to and returned from their picket line.*

Brigadier General Lewis A. Grant, commanding the Vermont Brigade, noticed this vulnerability and claimed to personally take Getty, Wright, and then Meade out to the picket line to show them the practicality of staging an attack at this point. The Army of the Potomac commander agreed, but told the Vermonter to wait until Grant's planned operations commenced.

The enlisted men took special interest in the earthworks as well, with expectations that they would soon be called upon to take this position. A New Yorker found them "well protected by abatis" and declared that they "could not be captured in daylight."

In the meantime, South Carolina Major Hammond naively wrote to his wife on March 29, "All is quiet again however and I am preparing a garden." The officer fully expected for McGowan's Brigade to remain in position long enough to harvest his crop. But by the time his letter reached home, the Union army had already muddled the gardener's plans.

*   *   *

Having regained the strategic initiative with the recapture of Fort Stedman and new possession of the Confederate picket line on the western front, Grant held a conference at City Point on March 28 to discuss his plans for ending the war. He invited Generals Sherman, Sheridan, and Meade, as well as Admiral David D. Porter, to determine the best course to destroy the Confederacy.

On March 24, President Lincoln had arrived at City Point on the *River Queen* and docked at the wharf. After the party moved on board to brief the commander in chief, Sherman and Grant admitted that at least one more bloody battle must be fought, but it likely would be the last.

"Mr. Lincoln exclaimed, more than once, that there had been blood enough shed, and asked us if another battle could not be avoided," recalled Sherman. The generals stated that the matter lay outside their hands and depended on the willingness of Lee and Davis to come to peaceful terms. The President accepted their assertion and began detailing his plan for a peaceful reunification

The Peacemakers—
This 1868 painting by
George P.A. Healy depicts
the famed strategy session
aboard the *River Queen*. (whha)

at the close of hostilities. Sherman returned to his army inspired by Lincoln's devotion to heal the nation:

> *I know, when I left him, that I was more than ever impressed by his kindly nature, his deep and earnest sympathy with the afflictions of the whole people, resulting from the war, and by the march of hostile armies through the South; and that his earnest desire seemed to be to end the war speedily, without more bloodshed or devastation, and to restore all men of both sections to their homes.*

At Jones Farm

The March 25 battlefield west of Church Road is preserved by the Civil War Trust and is accessible via the Jones Farm Loop Trail that begins off Stop 4 along the Headwaters Trail at Pamplin Historical Park. Though a short hike is required to reach this site, visitors are rewarded with the opportunity to view the well-preserved rifle pits held by the Confederate pickets until March 25 and then refaced by the next day by the VI Corps.

Unfortunately, the area of fighting east of the road is now the site of a steel plant. McIlwaine Hill is marked by a helipad but can still be discerned from the southeast corner of the intersection of Church Road and Hoffheimer Way.

The Civil War Trust restored the ground in front of Fort Welch to its appearance in the spring of 1865. (ea)

GPS: N 37.18289 W 77.47992

Lewis Farm
and White Oak Road

CHAPTER FIVE

Before Ulysses S. Grant dared to risk a frontal assault against the still-imposing Confederate fortifications, he first turned to the ace in his sleeve: the return of the Phil Sheridan's cavalry from the Shenandoah Valley. Grant intended to deploy this mobile unit to operate past the Confederate right flank at Petersburg. After resolving the crisis at Fort Stedman, the Union commander set his eye on shutting down the Boydton Plank Road and South Side Railroad. Should Lee send a sufficient force to engage Sheridan, Grant promised to swiftly engage the diminished lines at Petersburg.

On March 27, Grant called upon the Army of the James under the command of Maj. Gen. Edward O. C. Ord to bolster his offensive. Ord sent three infantry divisions plus a cavalry division from their positions near Richmond to Hatcher's Run. Meanwhile Grant established his headquarters near Dabney's Mill to be closer to his operations.

On the morning of March 29, the Army of the Potomac began extending their lines to the southwest to assist Sheridan's cavalry as they rode for Dinwiddie Court House on the Boydton Plank Road. Major General Gouverneur K. Warren's V Corps moved for Gravelly Run on Vaughn Road, hoping to swing back up and cut the plank road. Meanwhile, the II Corps took position on the south bank of Hatcher's Run to support Warren.

Lee reacted to this growing threat by gathering all available reserves west of Petersburg. He directed Maj. Gen. George Pickett to bring his division to Sutherland Station on the South Side Railroad and link up with Fitzhugh Lee's cavalry to protect the road network leading north from Dinwiddie Court House. At the same

This aerial view shows the marshy ground captured by the VI Corps on March 25. (rm)

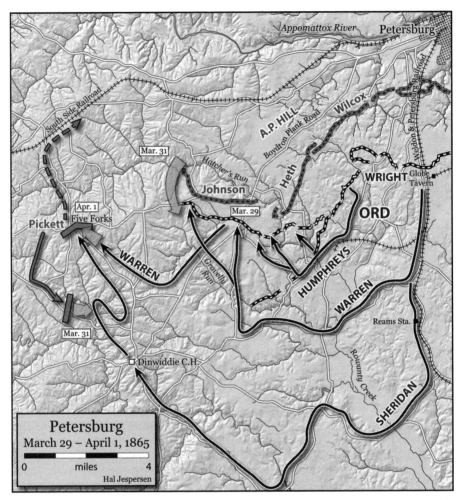

PETERSBURG: MARCH 29-APRIL 1, 1865—The narrow roads, flooded streams, and thick woods in Dinwiddie County proved to be a blessing for the Confederates in maintaining their fragile hold on the supply lines. The arrival of Ord's infantry and Sheridan's cavalry, however, provided Grant with the opportunity to finally engage the Confederates outside their fortifications.

time, Lt. Gen. Richard H. Anderson's undersized corps—consisting only of Maj. Gen. Bushrod R. Johnston's division—moved south from their fortifications anchored at Burgess Mill.

Their march brought them straight into an engagement with the V Corps that afternoon at Lewis Farm that would determine control of the Boydton Plank Road.

*   *   *

Around 3 p.m., Brig. Gen. Joshua Lawrence Chamberlain led the V Corps advance up Quaker Road.

As he passed Gravelly Run, his brigade slammed into Brig. Gen. Henry A. Wise's Virginians near a sawmill. The bluecoats pushed the Confederates back toward the Boydton Plank Road before a swift counterattack by Brig. Gen. William H. Wallace's South Carolinians stalled their drive. Brigadier General Charles Griffin added more of his division to the fray as both commanders escalated their efforts in the growing battle around the Lewis Farm. During the combat, Chamberlain suffered a painful wound and narrowly avoided capture before attempting to rally his men.

The arrival of the V Corps' artillery brought the Confederate assault to a halt. Colonel Charles S. Wainwright heard his cannons' influence from a distance: "I did not see it myself, but I realized the scene fully, for as I heard the first report, the rebel yell ceased, and the next moment our men hurrahed."

After two hours of fighting, Johnson's Division retired back to their entrenchments on the White Oak Road, losing 250 men. At the cost of 375 casualties, the V Corps now possessed the Boydton Plank Road. This tactical victory meant Grant had only to capture the South Side Railroad in order to isolate Petersburg. The Union army now stretched from the Appomattox River to Dinwiddie Court House.

Parke's IX Corps guarded the eastern side of Petersburg to the Jerusalem Plank Road. The VI Corps continued the line past the fishhook at Fort Welch. Ord's new arrivals occupied the II Corps' previous line between Wright and Hatcher's Run. Humphreys placed his three divisions south of Hatcher's Run parallel to Dabney's Mill Road, while Warren dug in on Boydton Plank Road. Sheridan's cavalry settled in five miles to the south around the courthouse.

* * *

That evening, Robert E. Lee instructed McGowan's Brigade to abandon their works near Tudor Hall and move south to extend the White Oak Road line. The South Carolinians suffered "a toilsome march through mud and rain and darkness" before reaching their camp. "We piled up great heaps of brush and fired them, and warmed ourselves to some sort of comfort," recalled a lieutenant.

In the swift move to relocate, McGowan had to leave his pickets opposite Fort Welch on duty in their rifle pits. With no additional reserves to commit, Wilcox ordered Lane's Brigade to merely extend their ranks south to plug the gap in the lines. "The men were placed from six to ten paces apart—a mere skirmish line," claimed one of Lane's officers.

After suffering a serious wound in the Wilderness in May, James Longstreet returned to command the First Corps in October. (php)

Joshua Lawrence Chamberlain claimed to deceive his would-be captors at Lewis Farm by speaking with a southern accent. (loc)

At White Oak Road, McGowan placed his command alongside Brig. Gen. William MacRae's North Carolinians, who also had to abandon their lines protecting the Boydton Plank Road in their shift to the south.

General Pickett also marched south that night on Claiborne Road from Sutherland Station to White Oak Road. The next morning, March 30, Lee gathered his commanders and detailed their placements. A visitor recalled the conference: "Lee on a broken fence the others round him while some officer is drawing a plan of the ground with a stick in the mud, all looking on while he described the position of the enemy Lee takes the stick & assigns to each Genl his position on the mud map."

Lee ordered Pickett to shift his division to the west and meet one of Fitzhugh Lee's divisions operating north of Dinwiddie Court House. The Virginian left Hunton's Brigade with Anderson in the fortifications but received two brigades from that command in exchange, bringing Pickett's total number of men to approximately 10,000. Colonel William J. Pegram joined the movement with his six pieces of artillery.

*   *   *

The heavy rains kept Sheridan close to Dinwiddie Court House on March 30. The general wanted to move for the Five Forks intersection to the northwest and the South Side Railroad three miles beyond, but the weather tempered his plans.

Sheridan frustratingly rode to Grant's headquarters to express his displeasure about the delay. He "chafed like a hound in the leash" before lashing out, "I tell you I'm ready to strike out tomorrow and go smashing things." Grant appreciated his cavalryman's enthusiasm and approved his idea to move forward as soon as possible.

The Union commander expected Sheridan's advance to be heavily contested: "It is natural to suppose that Lee would understand my design. . . . The roads were so important to his very existence while he remained in

The lengthy process of corduroying roads to allow for wagon passage delayed maneuvers through Dinwiddie County. (fl)

Richmond and Petersburg, and of such vital importance to him even in case of retreat, that he would make most strenuous efforts to defend them."

That afternoon, one of Sheridan's divisions advanced north before running into Confederate cavalry. The gray horsemen drove the Federal troopers back toward the courthouse. As they retreated, the Union cavalrymen noticed the arrival of Pickett's infantry to Five Forks around 4:30 p.m. The Confederates settled for the night south of the intersection and intended to attack the next morning.

Throughout the day, the Union infantry near Hatcher's Run strengthened their hold on Boydton Plank Road. Humphreys stretched his lines from Armstrong's Mill to the road where they connected with the V Corps. Warren's men pushed westward from the Lewis Farm battlefield through heavy woods and choked streams to a position nearly opposite Anderson's line on White Oak Road.

*   *   *

After gathering intelligence from scouts and Southern deserters, Meade decided to commit the VI and IX Corps into battle. "The enemy has undoubtedly weakened himself in your front," he wired Parke and Wright, instructing them to "attack at early daylight tomorrow."

Parke responded truthfully that he could not observe any changes of the enemy's position in his front but would still arrange an assault. Meanwhile, a heavy fog prevented Wright from determining the enemy's weakened strength opposite his men. The VI Corps commander reluctantly issued orders to attack but expressed his doubts to Meade.

Sheridan was not impressed with Dinwiddie Court House, calling it "a half-dozen unsightly houses, a ramshackle tavern propped up on two sides with pine poles, and the weather beaten building that gave official name to the cross-roads." (php)

Andrew Atkinson Humphreys took over command of the II Corps from Winfield Scott Hancock in November 1864. The most capable chief of staff the Army of the Potomac ever had, Humphreys had nonetheless longed for a field command. (loc)

After the Army of the Potomac's commander consulted with Grant that evening, he called off the assault but advised them to "keep a vigilant watch" and "take advantage of any opportunity presenting itself." By this time the rank-and-file of the VI Corps had already heard of their assignment and were now grateful to receive the latest update.

New Yorker Simon Cummins was happy about the cancellation, claiming to hear artillery being moved into position to receive the assault: "We was not much sorry either for we was a going to charge on a fort that had brass howitzers in and they would have been pretty apt to feed us some grape and canister." Second Lieutenant George O. French agreed that "there would have been dreadful slaughter."

Many realized the delay only represented a postponement of their inevitable orders and continued to meditate on their impending task. "We hope and pray that we may be able to strike the death blow of the rebellion," wrote Capt. Charles Morey in what tragically proved to be his last letter home to his mother. "Perhaps we may fail yet we hope for the best and will work hard for it and trust in God for the accomplishment of the reminder, now is the time that we need divine assistance, pray for us that we may accomplish all."

* * *

Charles Griffin commanded the Department of Texas after the war and firmly promoted a Radical Republican agenda during Reconstruction. (loc)

As Grant consolidated his position on March 31 and the VI Corps contemplated their future, Lee realized he must attack immediately to save Petersburg. He had already ordered Pickett to attack Sheridan. Now he wanted to drive Warren away from the White Oak Road before the V Corps could comfortably settle themselves in among the swampy forests and connect with the cavalry to the southwest.

Displaying his tendency for the offensive, Lee ordered four brigades out of their defensive positions to take advantage of the exposed Union left flank. If the Confederates rolled up the lead division of the V Corps, Lee could possibly force the Union entirely off the Boydton Plank Road.

McGowan's Brigade marched west of the Claiborne Road with orders to swing south and plunge into the Warren's flank and drive the Union corps to the east, while Bushrod Johnson's Division pitched in from the north.

About the same time, Warren had independently decided to seize the White Oak Road for himself and ordered Brig. Gen. Romeyn B. Ayres to advance his division. Johnson's men observed their pickets retreating and immediately charged, before McGowan was ready. "The boys in blue stood it for awhile, but finding that we were closing in for a hand-to-hand fight, they broke and ran, we at their heels yelling like devils, and burning powder for all we were worth," remembered a Virginian.

With all Union attention focused to the north, McGowan found the perfect opportunity to slam into their distracted left flank. "Before many seconds we immediately struck the enemy and charged them, cheering as was our custom, and pouring a rapid volley into their ranks," recalled Lt. James Caldwell. "The assailants, thus vigorously assailed, were smitten with dismay, and gave back rapidly, while we pressed on and drove them clear into open ground."

Warren ordered Brig. Gen. Samuel W. Crawford's division forward but they could not stem the tide. Instead their arrival merely provided additional targets for the elated attackers. "I have no idea that the brigade ever killed more men . . . than it did this day," claimed Caldwell. "Line after line fairly melted before them and dissolved into a heterogeneous mass of rabble."

Robert E. Lee's nephew Fitzhugh took command of the Army of Northern Virginia's cavalry for the final campaign. (php)

Soon Crawford's line also broke and ran back to Gravelly Run. As he watched his colleague's divisions stream into his lines, Brig. Gen. Charles Griffin angrily swore, "The Fifth Corps is eternally damned." Three Southern brigades had successfully routed two Union divisions.

The Confederates found the V Corps reserve line along Gravelly Run "posted on a hill whose sides were tangled and precipitous, and between which and us opened a ravine of considerable depth and unsafe footing." Unwilling to risk further losses, McGowan called a halt while the cowering remnants of Ayres's and Crawford's division recuperated behind Griffin's entrenched line. Meanwhile, Warren pleaded for assistance.

Major General Andrew A. Humphreys deployed Brig. Gen. Nelson A. Miles's division from the II Corps to attack the White Oak Road line. Miles's men immediately ran into Wise's Virginians, just beginning their movement southward, and pushed them back into their earthworks. This reversal isolated the three Confederate brigades to the west and forced them to return back to the position they originally captured from Ayres.

Ohio-born Bushrod Rust Johnson was one of few Northern natives who served as Confederate generals. (loc)

Warren sent Griffin's division forward to reclaim this ground. Ayres supported his left while Crawford connected the corps to Miles. This combined force pushed the Confederates all the way back to the White Oak Road.

Warren longed to further redeem his corps' reputation with an assault against the Confederate line and moved forward with his skirmishers under artillery fire to scout the enemy's earthworks. What he found quickly discouraged his hopes. "The enemy's defenses were as complete and as well located as any I had ever been opposed to," he reported and decided not to sacrifice any more of his men in a frontal charge. He did manage to secure a lodgment on the White Oak Road west of Anderson's line.

By the end of the fighting on March 31, the Union army suffered 177 killed, 1,134 wounded, and 554 missing, with Confederate losses likely totaling around 800. Warren's unsteady grip on the White Oak Road near its intersection with Claiborne Road in the aftermath of the battle now isolated Pickett's Division, which had done plenty of fighting of their own that day, four miles to the west.

At White Oak Road

GPS: N 37.15187 W 77.54972

Much of the Lewis Farm battlefield maintains its wartime appearance, but no portions of the battlefield are officially preserved or accessible to visitors.

The Civil War Trust preserves 898 acres of the White Oak Road battlefield, including the original Confederate fortifications near the Claiborne Road intersection. A two-thirds of a mile long interpretive trail allows visitors to follow the earthworks defended by Johnson's Division as well as view the ground contested between Wise and Miles. Six wayside exhibits orient visitors to the fighting in the area from March 29-April 2, 1865. Most of the ground covered by McGowan's Brigade in their assault is located on private property. Griffin's defensive line behind Gravelly Run is preserved, though currently not accessible.

OPPOSITE: **Confederate artillery position north of White Oak Road preserved by the Civil War Trust.** (ea)

Dinwiddie Court House and Five Forks

CHAPTER SIX

Owning a military career defined by disaster, George E. Pickett surprisingly enjoyed profound success on March 31, routing six brigades of Phil Sheridan's cavalry in piecemeal fashion.

Pickett left Col. Thomas T. Munford's cavalry division at Five Forks and instructed them to advance in conjunction with his movements to the south. At 10:00 a.m., Pickett took his infantry to the southwest to cross a small stream known as Chamberlain's Bed and strike Sheridan's left flank. By 2:00 p.m., the Confederates were in place. Pickett also established contact with the two cavalry divisions operating west of Dinwiddie Court House. He ordered them to seize Fitzgerald's Ford to the south while the infantry attempted a crossing at Danse's Ford to advance toward Courthouse Road.

Sheridan sent two brigades to contest the crossing, but Pickett easily stormed across Chamberlain's Bed and pushed the Union cavalry at the northern ford back toward Courthouse Road. Two more Union brigades rode up to slow Pickett but were compromised by Munford's arrival from the north.

Fearing that Pickett's infantry would continue their eastward movement and lend their weight to Warren's developing battle at White Oak Road, Sheridan sent two of his reserve brigades north from Dinwiddie Court House to engage the Confederates. For two hours, they fought along Courthouse Road until Pickett forced the units back in retreat.

Sheridan now called upon Brig. Gen. George Armstrong Custer—whose men spent the afternoon guarding the wagon trains south of the county seat—to cover the withdrawal. Custer set up a defensive line

Courthouse Road, Scott's Road, and Ford's Road all intersected into White Oak Road at Five Forks, making the location a critical strategic junction below the South Side Railroad. (ea)

north of Dinwiddie Court House and rallied the routed brigades on his flanks.

With the sun beginning to set, Pickett hoped to still drive the Union troopers from the crucial intersection near Dinwiddie Court House and prepared to launch one more assault. He instructed Fitzhugh Lee to sweep in on the left flank while his division attacked the Federal center. This final charge temporarily bent Custer's line but could not break it.

Sheridan lost 40 killed, 254 wounded, and 60 missing on March 31, while Pickett lost approximately 400 of his infantry and 360 of Lee's cavalry in driving the Union mounted arm back to Dinwiddie Court House.

The idea of personally besting Phil Sheridan so enthralled George Pickett that he planned a shad bake for the next day, April 1, to bask in his success. But Warren's position on the White Oak Road near the Burgess Mill line forced Pickett to withdraw his command back to the Five Forks intersection to try and restore communications with the rest of the army.

The first telegram received dampened Pickett's mood. "Hold Five Forks at all hazards," instructed Lee. "Protect the road to Ford's Depot and prevent Union forces from striking the Southside Railroad." The gray commander continued by chastising his subordinate: "Regret exceedingly your forced withdrawal, and your inability to hold the advantage you had gained."

Nevertheless Pickett continued to plan his festivities for the next day and personally withdrew north of Hatcher's Run, even as Sheridan stewed on his loss. Despite his tactical defeat on March 31, the feisty cavalryman saw great opportunity to even the score with Pickett's men. "This force is in more danger than I am," he declared, "if I am cut off from the Army of the Potomac, it is cut off from Lee's army, and not a man in it should ever be allowed to get back to Lee."

Sheridan had finally achieved Grant's goal that dated

back to the start of the Overland Campaign in May 1864: "We at last have drawn the enemy's infantry out of its fortifications, and this is our chance to attack it."

*   *   *

After falling back to his final position around Dinwiddie Court House, Sheridan requested infantry support. Grant could provide the V Corps, but did so with specific instructions to keep a close eye on General Warren.

Since his arrival to Virginia, Grant had been dissatisfied with Warren's performance. "He was a man of fine intelligence, great earnestness, quick perception, and could make his dispositions as quickly as any officer, under difficulties where he was forced to act," admitted Grant, but those came with a downside. "He could see every danger at a glance before he had encountered it."

Grant was concerned that Lee's army would slip away to the west. He needed commanders in place who would act swiftly and continuously press the opponent while all the pieces of the Union strategy to capture Petersburg and its defenders fell into place. "As much as I liked General Warren, now was not a time when we could let our personal feelings for any one stand in the way of success," Grant recalled, "and if his removal was necessary to success, not to hesitate."

Grant provided Sheridan with authorization to remove Warren should his movements once more prove to be too slow. Meanwhile, he instructed Warren to move at once to Dinwiddie Court House. The V Corps commander carefully extracted his men from their lines opposite the White Oak Road. As some units did not move until 5 a.m. the next morning, Warren received new instructions to march cross-country to the west to strike the Confederates at Five Forks on their left flank.

Pickett's men lined the White Oak Road for nearly a two-mile-long front centered on the star-shaped crossroads at Five Forks. Cavalry held either flank, and Colonel Pegram scouted open spots along the road to place his artillery. The Confederate left flank was refused back from the road, creating a short angle on that end of the line.

Sheridan's battle plan called for his dismounted troopers to use their repeating weapons to engage this thin line near the intersection. With the Confederates immobile behind their makeshift fortifications, the V Corps would sweep around their left flank, driving them to the west and away from the bulk of the Army of Northern Virginia. With that maneuver accomplished, the tracks of the South Side Railroad—Petersburg's final supply line—would lay open for the taking.

An accomplished engineer and the "Hero of Little Round Top" at Gettysburg, Gouverneur Kemble Warren struggled as a corps commander. (loc)

*   *   *

While Union cavalry popped away at the Confederate front, Warren marched his corps into position for the decisive sweeping attack. He instructed Ayres to advance up Gravelly Run Church Road to strike Pickett's left flank where he believed it to be at the intersection with White Oak Road. Meanwhile, he ordered Crawford's division on their right to work its way around the angle to roll the Confederate flank. Warren kept Griffin's men in reserve.

Sheridan, however, did not provide an accurate location regarding Pickett's position. The angle in the works was 700 yards farther west from where Warren believed it lay. Heavy woods prevented the V Corps general—already operating under close scrutiny—from properly scouting the position out on his own. Yet the time still dragged by for Sheridan as he bitterly awaited the infantry's delayed assault. Finally at 4 p.m., Warren signaled the movement forward.

Stubborn Confederate resistance on their right and center against Sheridan's cavalry made Warren's attack to the east the critical component of the battle. (hw)

As Crawford's men piled out of the woods near Gravelly Run Church, they completely missed the Confederate line half a mile to the west and pressed on across White Oak Road. The division plunged back into the undergrowth and continued on toward Hatcher's Run but away from their objective. Ayres also did not strike any Confederates as he moved astride the road but came under an enfilading fire from dismounted cavalry and artillery at the angle.

Warren frantically sent couriers to Crawford to correct his stray path. Frustrated by the lack of a response, he rode off after the wayward division leaving Ayres to realign his men along the road. Meanwhile Griffin marched behind Crawford's rear to the left in support of Ayres, whose division struggled under the heavy fire and dense undergrowth to work its way toward the angle. "Bullets were now humming like a swarm of bees about our heads, and shells were crashing through the ranks," remembered an officer.

Among the confusion, Sheridan rushed in among the advance units of the scattered V Corps and shouted, "Where is my battle-flag!" Seizing it from his color sergeant, the

Sheridan, who led the charge against the Angle, believed that it should have been Warren leading from the front. (hw)

diminutive cavalryman stood high in his saddle, waved the banner over his head, and cheered the infantry on. General Ayres also drew his saber and rushed forward, leading his men with fixed bayonets over the earthworks at the angle and capturing a number of prisoners.

Sheridan bounded over the earthworks behind the infantry and landed among the captives. He ordered them to head for the rear after relinquishing their weapons, declaring, "You'll never need them any more."

Throughout this attack, the dismounted cavalry continued to press the Confederate center and right. Pegram's artillery at the intersection rapidly fired double rounds of canister at close range as the Union troopers pressed within 30 yards of Five Forks. Learning of the crisis in the middle of the line, Pegram hurriedly galloped to the crossroads and loudly encouraged his cannoneers: "Fire your canister low, men!" A few moments later, the young colonel fell mortally wounded from his saddle.

Despite all the commotion, an acoustic shadow prevented Pickett, back above Hatcher's Run enjoying his shad planking, from hearing the noise of battle that signaled the collapse of his line.

The dismounted cavalry soon swarmed up to the makeshift Confederate fortifications and engaged in a vicious, though brief, hand-to-hand struggle. As Federal troopers closed in around Pegram's guns, an artilleryman at the muzzle swung his sponge-rammer at the first bluecoat to spring over the works.

Willie Pegram had previously motivated his command by declaring: "Men, whenever the enemy takes a gun from my battery, look for my dead body in front of it." His words became prophetic. (va.hs)

At this moment, the rerouting of the V Corps proved beneficial. Crawford's lost division worked their way around behind Pickett's line and gained possession of Ford's Road, enabling them to now strike the crumbling position at Five Forks from the rear. Cut off from direct retreat north to Hatcher's Run, only a stout defense by Fitzhugh Lee's cavalry on the Confederate right against repeated attacks by Custer prevented total disaster and allowed the tattered remains of Pickett's command to escape to the northwest. They crossed over Hatcher's Run upstream, having suffered 3,000 casualties, many of those being captured.

With just over 800 casualties, the Union now had an uncovered route to the South Side Railroad. Warren happily rode to meet with Sheridan to discuss the next day's plans to sever that supply route. A courier intercepted the general with a crushing dispatch: "Major-General Warren, commanding, Fifth Army Corps, is relieved from duty." Ever since the Overland Campaign, Sheridan had grown irreparably frustrated by Warren's slow marches and finally had Grant's approval to make the change. Charles Griffin took command of the corps.

*   *   *

Colonel Horace Porter of Grant's staff spent April 1 with Sheridan sending messages back to the Union commander. With the action at Five Forks wrapped up, he frantically rode back to Dabney's Mill with his exciting news. Upon reaching Grant's headquarters just

Horace Porter stayed by Grant's side after the war, serving as his personal secretary in the White House. (loc)

before 9 p.m., he found the general sitting with most of his staff around a fireplace, still oblivious to the recent developments on the far left flank. "He wore his blue cavalry overcoat, and the ever-present cigar was in his mouth," remembered Porter.

The colonel brimmed with enthusiasm to deliver his report and threw himself off his horse and rushed up to the general and vigorously slapped him on the back to the amusement of the rest of the party circling the fire. Porter recalled they broke out in further joy when he informed Grant of Sheridan's victory: "For some minutes there was a bewildering state of excitement, and officers fell to grasping hands, shouting, and hugging each other like school-boys."

As the staff officers roundly exchanged their congratulations, Grant scarcely uttered a word. The general asked how many prisoners Sheridan captured before walking back into his tent to scribble dispatches for all his subordinates on the Richmond-Petersburg front.

With the orders sent out over the wire, the commander walked back up to the joyful campfire and coolly stated: "I have ordered a general assault all along the lines."

At Dinwiddie Court House

Though most of the Dinwiddie Court House battlefield remains undeveloped, it is not officially preserved by any organization. The 1851 courthouse building still stands and was used by the county through 1998. A small granite marker stands on its grounds in memoriam to the Union and Confederate soldiers killed in the March 31 engagement and lists the many battles fought in the county during the Petersburg campaign. This monument, erected July 31, 1972, by the Confederate Memorial Association of Dinwiddie County, inaccurately claims that the last rebel yells were heard during this battle. Nearby signs placed by the Virginia Department of Historic Resources bring attention to the nearby birthplaces of Gen. Winfield Scott and former slave turned Mary Todd Lincoln confidant Elizabeth Keckley.

GPS: N 37.07788 W 77.58686

At Five Forks

Despite its important status as a catalyst for the fall of Petersburg, the Five Forks battlefield was not acquired by the National Park Service until 1990. Today, the organization preserves more than a thousand acres around the crossroads. A visitor center, opened in 2009 on Courthouse Road, offers an orientation to the area and should be consulted to walk, bike, or horseback ride the eight miles of trail spread across the battlefield.

A street sign pays tribute to the last supper of the Confederacy. (ea)

GPS: N 37.13952 W 77.62307

The site of Pickett's diversion during the combat is not preserved but is located near the appropriately named Shad Bake Lane off of Courthouse Road north of Hatcher's Run. Pickett, like Warren, should have been relieved from duty after his disappearance at Five Forks. Lee issued orders to relieve the disgraced general from his command, but apparently the command never reached Pickett. A few days later as Lee watched Pickett ride past, he turned to a staff officer and icily remarked, "Is that man still with this army?"

The VI Corps Prepares to Charge

CHAPTER SEVEN

Colonel Porter of Grant's staff celebrated the victory at Five Forks as the "beginning of the end" and the "reaching of the last ditch." But that climb was still someone's cross to bear, and the general in chief now hoped the VI Corps men could carry it forward.

Major General Horatio G. Wright already had specific instructions for his three division commanders as he prepared his men for the attack. He had anticipated Grant's orders and prepared to deploy his men with instructions similar to those from their cancelled attack on March 31. He arranged the corps into a wedge-shaped formation: Brig. Gen. George W. Getty's division in the center, guiding the assault, with Brig. Gen. Truman Seymour on his left and Brig. Gen. Frank Wheaton on his right. Each formed their brigades in deep columns with a single regiment front.

These eight brigades contained some of the best troops to call on for a frontal assault. In a four-year war chock full of ill-calculated and poorly-executed attacks, the VI Corps distinguished themselves for their prowess at the bayonet charge.

On May 3, 1863, they used their superior numbers to finally unseat the Confederates from behind their comfortable position along the stone wall at the base of Marye's Heights in the second battle of Fredericksburg.

On November 7, 1863, at the battle of Rappahannock Station, two brigades of the corps stormed rifle pits held by a similar number of Confederates in a rare nighttime assault that brought overwhelming success.

The following May, Col. Emory Upton utilized the capture of the Confederate picket line at Spotsylvania to creep close to Rebel fortifications before driving over

Fort Welch stood at the far western end of the fishhook in the Union lines. (rm)

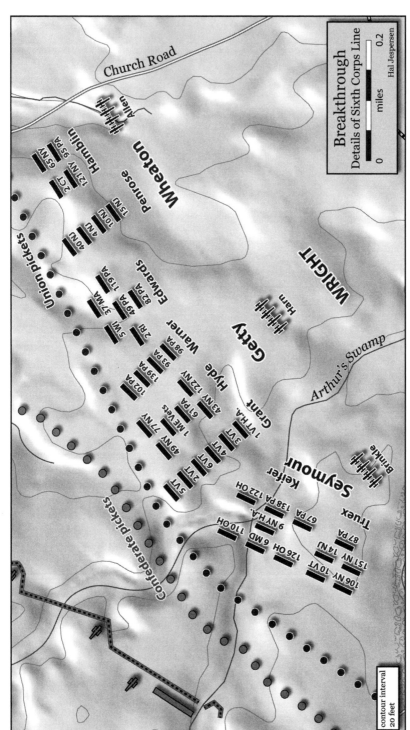

BREAKTHROUGH—Details of Sixth Corps Line: The compact formation adopted by Wright was rarely used during the Civil War due to its degree of difficulty. Early detection by the Confederates and the resulting concentrated artillery fire could tear the Union lines to pieces. The advantage, though, offered the chance to concentrate tremendous power against a single point.

Seven of Adams's Rhode Island artillerymen were awarded the Medal of Honor for accompanying the infantry charge. (php)

their entrenchments in a compact formation—all before the enemy really knew what hit them.

General Wright hoped to utilize all three of these advantages—numbers, visibility, and speed—on the morning of April 2.

Recent intelligence obtained from the advanced picket line captured on March 25 allowed Wright to carefully select a point in front of Fort Welch for the center brigade to focus on. A slight ravine ran directly to the Confederate works. "The ravine was previously covered with timber, which had been cut for fuel during the winter, the stumps and brush remaining, with more or less water in the lower places," described a Vermonter who noticed its vulnerabilities. "At a point where the ravine passed through, there was an opening in the Confederate works of about fifty feet."

Early detection of the massed columns would doom the assault. Wright included a stern warning in his circulated orders: "The necessity of perfect silence in this movement up to the time of making the assault cannot be too strongly impressed upon the command." He advised the front ranks not to load their weapons. Some officers took great pains to check that each soldier's weapon had not been primed with a percussion cap. Success of the movement would rely upon secrecy, speed, and the sharp steel of the bayonet.

Captain George W. Adams of Battery G, First Rhode Light Artillery, offered a section of his men to advance with the infantry carrying only their artillery implements to turn any captured pieces on the fleeing foe. Wright warned Adams of the extreme danger but approved the daring proposal. The captain returned to his battery hoping to find 20 volunteers. "It was a dangerous enterprise," admitted one of the cannoneers, "but the men were eager for a trial." Seventeen Rhode Island artillerymen stepped forward to participate. "We had brought with us lanyards, sponge-staffs, and

A company commander stated that James Hubbard had an "excited but calm determination in his eyes" the night before the breakthrough. (php)

Thomas Worcester Hyde stated that his pickets determining the weak spot on the enemy line illustrated "the cleverness of the American private soldier." (php)

such other tools as we thought might be necessary," remembered one. "It was a grand undertaking."

Some officers hoped to obtain one last bit of intelligence to help ease their way to the fortifications. Colonel Hyde learned from his pickets about an opening in the Confederate abatis leading to the wall. His scouts claimed that the enemy used this gap to cut and gather firewood and to go on picket. Furthermore, they noticed a large campfire stationed just behind the opening to guide the weary sentries in at night. "If we should direct ourselves on that fire we could get through the abattis easily," the colonel concluded.

Hyde brought all his regimental commanders to the top of the signal tower to brief them on this development. Here they once more glanced upon the imposing works that had ominously haunted the VI Corps over the winter. They stood as imposing a target as ever. The cleared ground between the lines offered countless obstacles to slow the attackers while they fell under fire.

"Along and in front of the line bristled a heavy fraise, a serried row of heavy sharpened stakes set close together and pointing outward with an unyielding and aggressive air, as if to say, Come and impale yourselves on us," remembered one of Getty's staff. How would the officers motivate their men to storm this line once operational control transferred down the chain of command?

Colonel Oliver Edwards pulled aside his regimental commanders and told them that they must succeed; failure endangered the whole army. Lieutenant Colonel Elisha H. Rhodes, commanding the 2nd Rhode Island, felt the pressure of the situation and chronicled in his diary that night: "The strain on our nerves is severe, and I feel that the soon the suspense is ended, the better. . . . Our officers and men have anxious looks. I have made every preparation, and have written what may be my last letters." Colonel Edwards noticed his nervous subordinate's concern and pulled Rhodes aside to joke, "Give them tomorrow what Paddy gave the drum, a good beating."

"Gentleman, we are going to have a hell of a fight at early daylight," Col. James Hubbard bluntly informed the company commanders of his 2nd Connecticut Heavy Artillery. "Now you can go to your quarters and if any of you have anything to say to your folks, wives or sweethearts make your story short and get what sleep you can for hell will be tapped early in the morning. . . . God only knows how many of us will ever come out of this damned fight. Good night, gentlemen, hoping our forces may be successful."

Hubbard's concerns had merit. Wright left little optimism in his assessment of his corps' objective point:

The works in front of the chosen point of attack were known to be an extraordinarily strong line of rifle pits, with deep ditches and high relief, preceded by one or two lines of abatis . . . a line of very strong fraise existed between them. At every few hundred yards of this line were forts or batteries well supplied with artillery. These lines might well have been looked upon by the enemy as impregnable, and nothing but the most resolute bravery could have overcome them.

Wright instructed pioneers to move in front of the columns to remove some of the obstacles that could slow the attack and doom its chances. "We were furnished axes, and instructed when the word 'Forward!' was given to push ahead and cut an opening for the storming column through the abatis," remembered a New York pioneer who noted two different kinds of obstructions, "common gut-punchers" and "rolling sawbucks." He also described "a network of telegraph wire 18 inches high from the ground."

Second Lieutenant George O. French recognized the importance of personal bravery to motivate his men to advance across this carefully prepared killing field. His company of the 1st Vermont Heavy Artillery faltered in combat on March 27—chased off McIlwaine Hill by the Confederate sharpshooters—and now he called on them to not shame themselves, their comrades, or their state with cowardice. "I will ask you to go nowhere that I do not go first," he declared, "and if I die, go on over my dead body, but go on."

Despite his assurances, a fellow company commander found plenty of problems with their objective:

First, it was so nearly dark that we could not see where we were going, next, immediately in front of our Brigade were two batteries whose fire we expected every moment

George Oscar French concluded his last letter home by mentioning how much he was enjoying reading Charles Dickens' *David Copperfield.* (va.hs)

While the Confederates lacked infantry manpower, their earthworks bristled with Third Corps batteries in well-prepared positions. (ea)

"During the remaining hours of that memorable night I paced my lonely beat, watching the lightening flashing guns, the glittering trajectory of the shells, and the fitful glare of their explosion, listening eagerly to every sound, striving to divine the position of my comrades, while equally intent that no danger should unexpectedly assail me." (fl)

to receive, thirdly, there were two lines of abatis which looked from a distance to be very formidable . . . fourthly, were the breastworks which were of considerable strength and for the fifth reason and the strongest of them all, we expected to find them completely lined with men ready to deal death and destruction to us.

Across the field, Col. William J. Martin of the 11th North Carolina viewed the Confederate line with a lesser assessment. He claimed the earthworks "would have been impregnable if defended by any adequate force," but sadly reported that they were occupied "by a mere skirmish line." Nursing a wound from the previous September, Martin returned to his regiment the day before the battle and found them in position just in front of Mrs. Hart's house south of the lower branch of Arthur's Swamp.

To his right lined up the 52nd North Carolina, also of MacRae's Brigade. With the bulk of the brigade transferred down to Hatcher's Run with their commander, Swedish-born Lt. Col. Eric Erson commanded the two regiments.

To their left stretched Lane's Brigade from the lower branch of Arthur's Swamp to where they met Thomas's Brigade near Church Road. Brigadier General James H. Lane had also just returned to command from an absence. He deployed his North Carolina infantry regiments, from right to left, Capt. Thomas J. Linebarger's 28th, Lt. Col. John W. McGill's 18th, Maj. Jackson L. Bost's 37th, and Col. Robert Cowan's 33rd.

*   *   *

Around 10:00 p.m., Union batteries stringing from Fort Gregg to the Appomattox River east of Petersburg erupted in fire. Around 150 guns lent their weight to the bombardment that lasted until 1:00 a.m. "I have never seen so many shells in the air at one time as then," wrote a Vermont captain. "It being quite dark they could be seen very distinctly describing their brilliant and terrible curves."

A musician in the 126th Ohio claimed:

Never in the history of time was such firing heard on this side of the Atlantic. Those miles and miles of huge engines of war seemed fairly to leap into the air, the very earth beneath quaking and trembling at each discharge of these war monsters which sent shot and shell into the enemy's camp so rapidly that there was a constant flash as of lightning in intense darkness. . . . Never, to my dying day, shall I forget that sublime, fearful, magnificent spectacle, which no brush could paint or pen describe.

The VI Corps used the cover of this bombardment to deploy in front of Fort Welch for their charge. Getty positioned Brig. Gen. Lewis Addison Grant's Vermont Brigade in the lead, instructing him to follow the Arthur's Swamp ravine to the Confederate fortifications. To their right in echelon waited Col. Thomas Worcester Hyde's brigade. "My first thought after getting the brigade in position was to look for the camp-fire that was to be our bright beacon," remembered the youngest brigade commander in the corps. "There it was shining peacefully through the mist."

Colonel James Meech Warner placed four Pennsylvania regiments into position to Hyde's left-rear, leaving the 62nd New York behind to garrison the forts.

Wheaton's First Division continued the VI Corps' wedged line to the right, with Col. Oliver Edwards's brigade supporting Warner. Edwards detailed 75 volunteers from the 37th Massachusetts—all armed with Spencer repeating rifles—to cover the brigade's assault once the firing began.

Colonel William Henry Penrose's once-reliable New Jersey Brigade waited beside Edwards. The Garden Staters' ranks were thinned from heavy casualties and expired terms. Rather than integrating new recruits into veteran units, state officials decided to raise a brand new regiment chock full of untrustworthy conscripts to send to the front. Penrose selected this unit—the 40th New Jersey—as the forlorn hope in his front line.

Colonel Joseph Eldridge Hamblin's brigade composed the right end of the column. The colonel arranged his four veteran brigades in two ranks.

Truman Seymour, commanding the Third Division, positioned Col. Joseph Warren Keifer's brigade to the left of Getty's men. One of his Ohio soldiers worried about what lay ahead. "Will there be an avenue leading up to the rebel works wide enough for a man's body that will not be pierced from end to end with balls, grape,

"If there were ever an instance when bayonets did think," surmised Lewis Addison Grant, **"it was when in the hands of the Old Vermont Brigade."** (na)

LEFT: "Rough and exacting in the extreme," George Washington Getty expertly led his division as a career officer. CENTER: Frank Wheaton previously distinguished himself on July 12, 1864, for his command at Fort Stevens in the defense of Washington. RIGHT: The weak link among the VI Corps division commanders from his mismanagement at Olustee and the Wilderness, Truman Seymour spent his retirement in Europe as a prolific watercolor painter. (php)(php)(hw)

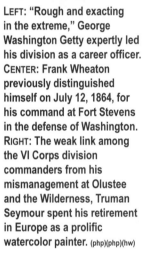

canister, and all the deadly solids that can be stuck into the hollow teeth of that big iron fine-comb?" asked the nervous private. "Yes," comforted his corporal, "but it will not be lower than the level of the clouds."

On the far left, Col. William Snyder Truex formed his five regiments close to the Confederate sentries in front of the Hart house. "The troops were placed in position without attracting the attention of the enemy, although within 150 yards of its picket-line," he reported.

At 11 p.m., Wright wired Meade: "Everything will be ready. The corps will go in solid, and I am sure will make the fur fly."

*   *   *

After the Union attackers settled into place behind the Jones Farm rifle pits, the men still had an excruciatingly long wait before the signal gun's fire. "The night was very dark and cold. The ground was damp, and the men were almost benumbed to lay upon it, without fire or light," recalled a Vermonter.

Captain Darius J. Safford remembered the "terrible anxiety of those hours of waiting. . . . The night was cold, the ground wet from recent rains, but we were obliged to lay very close almost all the time." The hours crawled by, an unbearable pause for many. "I would rather charge than lie here in this suspense and misery," complained a New Yorker.

Through it all, the officers continued to remind their men of the need for silence, even as the Confederate pickets fired periodically into the darkness. "We were treated to the sensation of lying upon a field for a long time exposed to the fire of the enemy's skirmishers without any shelter," recalled Cpl. DeWitt C. Beckwith of the 121st New York Infantry. "Every once in a while some one would get hit with a ball, and we could hear his cry of anguish as the lead tore through." The Northerners had to muffle the wounded to avoid detection. "This was a tough place to stay, with nothing to do but lie there and take our medicine," remembered a young Wisconsin soldier.

Losses took their toll among the Union leadership during these sporadic barrages. Colonel Erastus D. Holt of the 49th New York—who declared at the start of the war, "I am not good for much, but I may be instrumental in doing some good for the old Stars and Stripes. I was born under that glorious banner and, so help me God, I will die under it or in fighting for its defense,"—fell mortally wounded during the night. Colonel John W. Crosby was also hit from the picket fire. His fourth wound of the war proved to be mortal, marking the nineteenth officer in the 61st Pennsylvania to be killed in battle—the most among the Union army.

The officers had wisely instructed their men not to load their weapons so that no trigger-happy soldier would give away their concealed position. "Our men were constantly being hit without an opportunity to retaliate," recalled Crosby's successor, Maj. Robert L. Orr. "This inability to return the enemy's fire is misery intensified to the soldier."

Another bullet struck Lewis Grant in the head, threatening to unravel the VI Corps plan before the attack even stepped off. The Vermont general survived his wound but passed command of the lead brigade on to Lt. Col. Amasa Sawyer Tracy.

To silence the fire before further noise or retribution revealed the massed columns, Union pickets shouted out, "April Fool, Johnnies," and soon the eerie quiet resumed along the lines.

The Vermonters Break Through

CHAPTER EIGHT

General Wright had selected 4 o'clock to begin the assault, but as the time rolled around he determined "the unusual darkness at that hour rendered any connected movement impracticable." He delayed until "it had become light enough for the men to see to step, though nothing was discernable beyond a few yards distance."

At 4:40 a.m., the 3rd Vermont Battery at Fort Fisher fired the signal, and 14,000 men rose, shook out their numbed limbs, and quietly marched for the walls.

"On we went, with our guns slung by the straps at our backs and our axes in hand," described a New York pioneer. Behind their advance, the entire VI Corps trudged forward through darkness. The men silently groped across the barren ground toward the Confederate sentries.

"No word was spoken, as they came upon and passed over the entrenched picket line," recalled Lt. Charles H. Anson as the Vermont Brigade hoped to quietly capture the rifle pits. "No sound broke the stillness until the enemy's pickets, conscious of some power advancing upon them like a might ocean wave, with unbroken crest, delivered their fire and ran to cover in disorder. Then went up a shout from twenty-five hundred loyal hearts, taken up and repeated by the on-coming host. The charge was on!"

With the Vermonters only a few hundred yards away from their objective along the main line, the rifle flashes from a few alert sentries betrayed their position, and an observer at Fort Welch witnessed the Confederate lines erupt in flame. For half a mile along the earthworks, he saw "a line of flashing fires, crackling, blazing and sparkling in the darkness, more vividly lighted up by

Trees now cover the once bare earthworks assaulted by the Vermonters at Pamplin Historical Park. (ea)

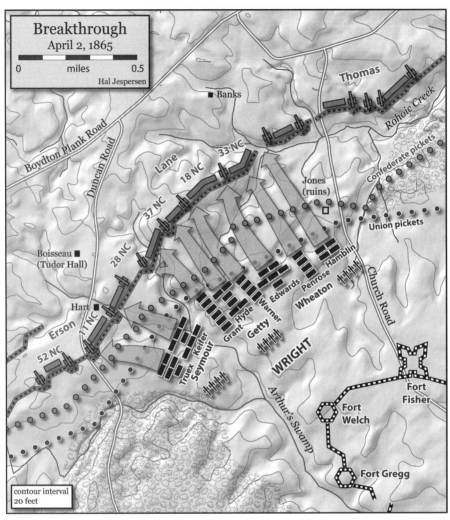

Breakthrough
April 2, 1865

BREAKTHROUGH—Approximately 14,000 Union soldiers in the VI Corps participated in the charge toward the Boydton Plank Road. The 2,800 Confederates from three Third Corps brigades would have to rely on the shock value of their bristling artillery fire combining with the delays from the obstructions and earthworks.

the heavier flashes of artillery, while shells, with their fiery trails, sped forward through the gloom in every direction."

Lieutenant Anson confirmed these fears:

> *Thick and fast came the cannon shot, thicker and faster came the bullets, when, for a moment, perhaps two, possibly ten, the charging column wavered, seemed to hesitate, the cannons' flashes lit up the terrible scene, revealing the struggling mass as it swayed to the right and left, recovering from the*

first great shock of battle. Were they, of whom so much was expected, to fail?

The sudden outburst attracted the attention of the North Carolina regiments stationed south of the Vermont Brigade's objective. "When their main column advanced and took most of our pickets, only a few escaped to bring the news that the Yankees were advancing," wrote a sergeant in the 11th North Carolina. "We directed our fire toward the noise, it not being light enough to see those in the front." Another in the regiment claimed, "I was shooting at Yanks in front of me where they were thick as black birds."

An Ohio axeman frantically working on removing the abatis recalled, "While we were doing this seven of our

The Vermont Brigade followed this branch of Arthur's Swamp, heavily inundated from the spring rains, to guide them to the Confederate works. (ea)

pioneer comrades were killed in that one place, it was dark but we were so close to their works that they could shoot us like rabbits."

By this time, the urgency for secrecy had passed, and the Union soldiers began to cheer as they strained forward. However, the anxiety had rendered the young Wisconsin soldier, Pvt. Clark F. Barnes, mute. "When I started on that charge I was not feeling very well; there was something the matter with my throat," he recalled. "I thought my heart would jump clear out of my mouth. The boys were yelling and charging all around me. I think I went more than half way across before I yelled, and then I felt so much better that I was sorry I had not yelled when I started. I was much surprised at the great change in my feelings. After that whoop I think I could have tackled the whole so-called Southern Confederacy."

These Confederate rifle pits, their fall back line after the battle of Jones Farm, stand just a few hundred yards in front of the main line. (ea)

As the attackers approached the rifle pits, some pickets threw down their guns and surrendered, shouting, "Don't fire, Yanks!" Others who had lost their enthusiasm for the Confederate cause called out, "Go on boys, they can't stop you." In an effort to swiftly continue the assault, the storming parties quickly disarmed their prisoners and ordered them to the rear on a run.

Vermonter Charles Henry Anson saw his wounded brigade commander show up later in the day with a bandaged head. (vt.hs)

Wright instructed the Vermonters to follow Arthur's Swamp into the Confederate earthworks, but the ravine veered slightly to the left just before it dissected the lines. There a battery situated directly to their right swung into position to deliver a devastating enfilade fire into the swamp.

Most of the brigade obliqued to the right out of the ravine hoping to find relief from the storm of lead. Someone in the rear cried out, "Bear to the left!" to correct them, but Capt. Charles Gilbert Gould, commanding Company H of the 5th Vermont still in the low ground, misunderstood that suggestion as a directive to himself and plunged across the swamp towards the left. "The officers rushed ahead without looking back to see whether the men were following," worried a Vermonter as only a handful kept Gould's pace approaching the earthworks. "I could not have run faster to save my life," another testified.

Gould briefly stopped to gather his men and found just a handful of officers and about 50 enlisted men still with him. The rest of the Vermonters had gone farther to the right on the other side of the swamp. The captain figured he would take his chances that some of Keifer's men might be in their vicinity to assist and rushed onward into the ditch and up the other side.

As the young lad deftly ascended to the top, he found himself hopelessly outnumbered. Upon reaching the parapet, he found a muzzle forced right into his chest. The Confederate musket misfired, but as the captain jumped into the works, another North Carolinian thrust up a bayonet that passed through Gould's lip and out his jaw. The stunned Vermonter "gave as good as he got" and managed to drive his own sword into his attacker and reached to pull the bayonet out of his bloody face. While in the process, another Confederate struck him on the head with a sword.

Just beyond this point in the last hundred yards of the charge, the ground drastically drops before a steep climb to reach the Confederate artillery emplacements. (ea)

Gould turned and grasped for the wall behind him but lacked the strength to pull himself into the relative safety of the ditch. While more North Carolinians bludgeoned the captain with clubbed muskets, Cpl. Henry Recor leapt over the wall and grabbed Charlie's arms to help him out. First Lieutenant Robert Pratt followed close behind in assistance and recalled: "Captain got a bayonet wound through cheek, a saber cut across his head, a bayonet wound in back &

stroke of a musket on the shoulder and across the breast, but while they were doing this he killed two of them."

The Confederates refused to let him go and seized the captain's coat and pulled him back, plunging another bayonet through his back. Recor fired into the Confederate mass and finally pulled the battered captain back over the wall. A piece of shell struck Recor below his left knee, shattering his leg, but he still managed to drag his captain into the ditch.

Miraculously, Gould survived his wounds and managed to crawl his way back to his own lines. "My part in the affair terminated long before daylight and was somewhat exciting to me personally," he drily wrote after the war. But at the time he defiantly declared if he only had his revolver he "could have held the fort alone."

Meanwhile, the few who kept pace with the youthful Vermont officer fought desperately to maintain their presence on the parapet. Sergeant Jackson Sargent scrambled up the slope and planted the state colors on the earthworks, sustaining a slight wound in the process. Immediately Cpl. Nelson E. Carle followed behind bearing the national flag. "Come on boys, the works are ours!" shouted Cpl. Charles A. Ford in encouragement as he dashed up the wall before a gunshot instantly killed him.

While the small band from the 5th Vermont frantically clung to their toehold, the next waves in the

Though it is hard to spot where Charles Gould first scaled the wall, it is believed to be somewhere in this vicinity at what is now Pamplin Historical Park. (ea)

Believed by his command to have "climbed the golden stairs," Gould recovered from his wounds and eventually received the Medal of Honor in 1890 for his actions. (php)

Just nineteen years old on April 2, 1865, Hawkins also received the Medal of Honor for his leadership during the breakthrough. (php)

Like many VI Corps regiments, the 93rd Pennsylvania claimed Charles Marquette was first to plant the colors on the works. The corps earned thirty-six Medals of Honor for their efforts on April 2. (php)

brigade continued to struggle through the abatis. As the 1st Vermont Heavy Artillery reached the first line of obstructions, a bullet struck Lieutenant French in the head, instantly killing him. Just as he had urged them the night before, his command pushed on over their dead officer's body.

Others began to waver, compelling Adjutant Gardner C. Hawkins of the 3rd Vermont to spring forward waving his sword and cheering his men onward until he reached the works and fell with a gunshot through the face. Remarkably, the 19-year-old survived his wound but refused to leave the field until his men reached the wall.

Some Vermonters worked their way laterally across the abatis fronting the earthworks until they finally found a gap in the obstructions used by the Confederate pickets to move in and out of the fortification. A cannon rolled temporarily into position to cover this narrow opening, threatening to annihilate this storming party. Lieutenant Pratt swiftly worked his way down the wall and, with his sword, cut down the gunner just before the cannoneer yanked the lanyard for one last point-blank shot into the swarming ranks.

"As the Union force passed over and into the enemy's works, a hand-to-hand struggle took place," wrote Lieutenant Anson. "Most desperately did the enemy defend their position, dealing blow for blow, fighting for, and over each gun, using the bayonet freely." A handful of officers made a stand to rally the men of the 37th North Carolina, but instead provided targets as the Vermonters now began to load and fire.

"After a stubborn resistance, we were overpowered and our lines taken," recalled 1st Lt. Octavius A. Wiggins, who received a gruesome scalp wound. While grappling with a Vermonter, the Union soldier fired errantly "in such close proximity to [my] head as to blow powder into [my] face, nearly destroying [my] eyes and knocking [me] senseless upon the ground." The North Carolinian awoke to find himself among a number of his command taken prisoner. Luckily his men succeeded in picking the powder out of his face and he soon regained his sight.

Once on the defenders' side of the earthworks, the Vermonters enjoyed a considerably easier time, and their numerical superiority quickly overpowered the Tarheels. A sergeant in the 5th Vermont recalled that they carried the works "at the point of the bayonet after a short but very fierce struggle." From their distant watch, the observers at Fort Welch noticed as the Confederate fire subsided: "Suddenly in the middle of it there appeared a tiny black spot, a narrow gap, which spread and widened, moment by moment, to the right and left."

With the enemy on the run, the attackers swiveled the cannon they left behind on them. Major William J. Sperry of the 6th Vermont had followed closely behind Gould and Pratt to the battery. After Pratt cut down the gunner, Sperry frantically searched for friction primers to use the field guns against the Confederates before they could rally. Unable to find one, he grabbed a musket and fired it into the vent, successfully igniting the piece. He continued in this manner until the detachment of volunteer artilleryman reached the scene with their implements. For his improvisation, Sperry later earned the Medal of Honor.

The efforts of this first band of Vermonters enabled successive waves to funnel in on the seized foothold and sweep up and down the lines.

*   *   *

Hyde's brigade formed in four lines to the right of the Vermonters. The colonel supplied the two lead New York regiments with axes and instructed them to remove the abatis while the rest of his command charged through. "Some confusion occurred on account of the intense darkness," he recalled, "but the colors of the different regiments and those directly about them, guided by the fire of the enemy, went straight on to their destination. Several regiments of the brigade claim their colors as first on the works, but the darkness must leave that honor forever undecided."

Major Robert L. Orr, commanding the 61st Pennsylvania in the third wave, claimed that his regiment suffered heavily "from the time we left the ground of formation until they fired in our faces and we tasted their smoke." While half the demoralized regiment fled back toward Fort Welch, the remainder pressed on and earned five Medals of Honor for bearing flags to the front while wounded or capturing a Confederate banner.

Two more New York regiments brought up the rear of Hyde's brigade. "When the bugles sounded the charge, we made a grand rush for the enemy's breastworks, they pouring in their shells like hail," wrote Lt. Col. Horace H. Walpole of the 122nd New York.

The confusing darkness caused many of the regiments in the narrow columns to intertwine. The 102nd Pennsylvania led the charge for Warner's brigade on the right of the Second Division. After they reached 75 paces, the 139th Pennsylvania stepped off. When the 102nd briefly halted at the abatis, the trail unit nearly slammed into their comrades. Major James McGregor, commanding the 139th, feared the blended attack would bog down in easy range of Confederate artillery. He ordered his color sergeants to press forward past the first

Robert Pratt's superior reported after the battle that he "added materially to his reputation of being a soldier in every sense of the word, as well as one of the most unequaled daring." (php)

With his regimental commander sick at the time, William Joseph Sperry commanded the 6th Vermont during the breakthrough. He reportedly fired twelve artillery rounds in his makeshift manner before turning the guns over to proper cannoneers. (php)

While en route to Johnson's Island prison, Octavius A. Wiggins leapt out of the train and made his way back to North Carolina. (php)

William Thorne Nicholoson, 37th North Carolina, was killed eight days after his brother's death at Fort Stedman. (php)

line with the hope that enough men would stick to the colors and continue on to the fortifications.

In his haste, Color Sgt. Charles Marquette of the 93rd Pennsylvania accidentally stumbled into the sharpened end of the abatis but continued to painfully hurry on. Despite starting from the third line, he was the first in the brigade to plant his flag on the earthworks. The 20-year-old received the Medal of Honor the following month for his work.

"The wedge which was to split the confederacy was driven home," claimed a jubilant observer.

Union artillery moved out of Fort Welch and the surrounding batteries to provide forward support and to stem potential Confederate counterattacks. (ea)

Expanding the Breach
CHAPTER NINE

Private David A. Christian of the 13th South Carolina fired frantically from his rifle pit, offering the Union attackers in his front a sterner response than the Vermont Brigade had experienced. Left behind during McGowan's move to Hatcher's Run, the Virginia native soon hung his ramrod in the gun with his rapid reloading. His comrade at the sentry post offered a selfish solution. "He suggested that he would load his gun and I would do the shooting. He was glad to do this as he could lie down in the pit. We fought this way for some time—an hour or more. I was fearful that my gun would burst if I attempted to shoot with the ramrod hung in the barrel but when the enemy came again, I reached my arm out as far as I could reach it and pulled the trigger and shot the ramrod at them."

Wheaton's division hit the Confederate earthworks just minutes after the Vermonters. As Edwards's brigade reached the trench, a Wisconsin private realized that it was too wide to jump across, so he dove in. "There were a few of the boys in the ditch then," he wrote, "and more were coming fast. I saw a comrade reach up and catch hold of a root. I boosted him, and up he went. I then caught the same root, and some one helped me."

The next waves in the brigade effortlessly reached the Confederate rifle pits but were held up in the obstructions. Fourteen-year-old William Wallace Perry led the way for his company as the 82nd Pennsylvania cleared the rifle pits: "They had a strong line of abatis and I being small got through all right. Our Color Sergeant threw the colors over to me." He raised the flag over his head and started to run for the earthworks, waving the flag, before the sergeant loudly cussed him

Mrs. Hart stayed in her house through the campaign, taking shelter in the cellar whenever the lines were shelled. (rm)

Private Christian's story seems the exception. Most Confederate pickets immediately fled upon detecting the assault or were instantly captured. (ea)

out to wait for the larger men to disentangle themselves from the snaring branches.

Lieutenant Colonel Elisha H. Rhodes halted the 2nd Rhode Island in the rifle pits and took a moment to scan his objective. He found a four-gun battery firing canister on the left and two guns to his right. The 23-year-old decided to split the gap before he found a wagon road to guide them to the works near the two-gun battery.

"The first I knew I fell into the ditch with a number of my men after me," remembered Rhodes. "The Rebels fired their cannon and muskets over our heads, and then we crawled up the rope and onto the parapet of their works, stepping right among their muskets as they were aimed over the work."

Inside the fortifications, Edwards's men battled in similar fashion as the Vermonters. "Just as I struck the ground inside several rebel guns flashed over the works a few paces to my right and a little farther on a cannon was fired," remembered the Wisconsin private. "There was a hot time here for a minute or two, and Orderly-Sergeant Yates Lacy was one of the boys who did a little artistic bayonet work, and the Johnny that he interview passed on to the sweet subsequently."

A small group of Rhode Islanders under 1st Lt. Frank S. Halliday swung to the left and charged the four-gun battery. The 30 men quickly captured three of the pieces, but Confederate artillerists managed to haul away the fourth. Halliday chased after the gun and captured it "with very little trouble."

Some of Lane's Brigade put up as stout of a resistance as their small numbers could allow. "They seemed to be distributed along the earthworks, in squads of three to six, and in no instance did I see any of them leave their posts until they had given us the contents of their muskets," recalled Halliday. "We fought desperately, but our thin line was pushed back by sheer force of numbers until it

Oliver Edwards, former colonel of the 37th Massachusetts, enjoyed their use of the Spencer Repeating Rifle in silencing batteries, writing "we have always found them our best and truest friend." (loc)

While these artillery positions offered the Confederates their only chance in this battle, their quick capture and repurposing doomed any opportunity for a counterattack. (rm)

was broken in pieces," claimed a North Carolinian. "We then retreated behind our winter quarters and continued the contest, each man for himself."

A squad of Confederates formed a line perpendicular to their works and rallied to reclaim the fourth cannon. The Rhode Islanders swung the captured piece on the Tarheels but could not find any artillery rounds. Their commander noted that the men "filled the gun to the muzzle with stones and fired it right in the faces of the Rebels." The gun burst as it fired, but Lieutenant Colonel Rhodes grimly reported: "The enemy made no more charges." The gruesome scene stuck with Halliday the rest of his life: "Such destruction of life I never saw, before or since."

To their right, Penrose's brigade struggled to reach the Confederates lines. As their commander expected, the 40th New Jersey performed poorly in the lead and broke three times before the next waves overtook them. The mingled regiments relied on the Spencer repeating rifle-armed 37th Massachusetts just to their left to help them over the works.

"A handful of men, under protection of their volley, found a standing place under the angle of a parapet, where they could not be reached by artillery or struck by the riflemen, unless they exposed themselves," wrote Chaplain Alanson Haines. "After a continuous volley of musketry a few would rush into the place, until there was a sufficient number to leap into the fort and carry it by assault."

The 18th North Carolina fought valiantly to the bitter end and refused to yield as the Jerseymen poured into the fort. "Our thin line could make but feeble resistance to the Sixth corps hurled against us," declared the regiment's adjutant, who claimed they detained Penrose's men until broken lines elsewhere doomed their efforts. As one private shouted that he would never surrender, a Union soldier sank a bayonet into

Son of an officer in the regular army and born in a New York barracks, William Henry Penrose had high expectations for his soldiers. (loc)

German immigrant Frank Fesq earned the Medal of Honor for his capture of the 18th North Carolina's flag. (php)

his torso. Private Frank Fesq, meanwhile, grappled with the regimental color bearer in a vicious hand-to-hand struggle and suffered a smashed hand and severe cut in his thigh. The Tarheel color bearer finally relinquished his flag after a nearby officer drew his pistol and wounded the determined lad.

* * *

Just to the north, Thomas's Georgia pickets anticipated an attack. Around 4 o'clock that morning, the skirmish line commander summoned Cpl. Joseph S. Kimbrough to advance out to the vidette post to investigate. The corporal expected to soon encounter the Union army and requested that his officer not allow the pickets to fire until he could return safely. After he crawled 200 yards in front of the line he observed, "I could hear distinctly the enemy in my front preparing for the charge." Kimbrough had likely arrived just shy of Hamblin's brigade on the far right flank of the VI Corps formation. Before he could report his findings, the cannon at nearby Fort Fisher signaled the attack.

The close proximity to the fort allowed the Union soldiers in Hamblin's brigade to trace the course of the signal gun's shell as it sailed through the sky at their objective. "We were up in another moment, in closed ranks, feeling for the man on our right we plunged forward in the darkness," wrote Pvt. DeWitt Clinton Beckwith. "A little farther on, and the Rebel works were marked by the jets of flame from their rifles as they fired upon us."

Corporal Kimbrough had to dodge this fire as he returned to his own men. While bullets "hissed above," he crawled on his hands knees back to his own sentry line where he "gave my excited comrades a piece of my mind in not very complementary terms." Before the Georgians could resolve their differences, the Union soldiers advanced on the earthworks to their right, which forced the small party to retreat to the northeast.

Hamblin's officers had taken extra precautions to provide large quantities of axes for the men to chop their way through the abatis. However, the paths of a few lucky New York soldiers took them straight to the opening in the tangled brush used by the pickets. "Here's a road!" they cried, and the Yankees ran straight for the artillery that would have had them pinned down in the obstructions. Reaching the ditch, they climbed up its sides and entered the Confederate fort through the one of the gun embrasures. "The bayonet and butt did the rest," claimed a New Yorker, who also noted that the men had trouble telling friend from foe in the darkness.

Wheaton's other two brigades had already reached

the fortifications to Hamblin's left and caused many of the Confederates to flee. The colonel welcomed just the token resistance. "Owing to the early hour and mist of morning, and the nature of the ground, the troops were in some confusion arriving at the rebel lines," he admitted as his four regiments tumbled over the earthworks. As easy as the arrival was, their stay proved more difficult.

With no more Union brigades on their right to offer support, his men took a terrible fire from the east. Two Napoleon cannons of the Norfolk Light Artillery Blues provided the warm reception. One of the Virginia artillerymen recalled that they took their guns out of the earthworks and "placed it in position to enfilade inside our own line." The artillery fire forced the Union soldiers to hug the Confederate walls. "Shells were yelling with the fierceness of demons let loose from the infernal regions," recalled a Connecticut corporal.

As Union commanders formed a mixed detachment to storm the pieces, the remnants of Lane's Brigade slammed through Thomas's Brigade, which joined the rush through the battery in retreat. "Our infantry were flying by our guns in a perfect panic," wrote a bitter gunner who claimed that the two pieces had to frequently hold their fire to allow their demoralized comrades to pass.

"By his many engaging qualities" Joseph Eldridge Hamblin "won the affection" of his men – "They loved, honored, almost idolized him." (loc)

"The heavy line of bluecoats was now drawing a fatal cordon around the devoted battery," recalled Kimbrough, whose group momentarily stopped to provide infantry support. Recognizing that "there was no shadow of a chance for a successful resistance," the Georgians continued their withdrawal. The battery soon fell and a handful of converted artillerymen among Hamblin's infantry soon worked the pieces against their former owners who also now fled.

Meanwhile, small Union parties plundered the Confederate camps while others worked their way independently toward the Boydton Plank Road and South Side Railroad looking for prizes or glory. Eventually, Wright ordered Hamblin to face his brigade perpendicular to the captured earthworks while he swung the rest of the corps to the south, past where Seymour's two brigades division had encountered heavy resistance that morning from Heth's Division.

A lawyer before the war, Joseph Warren Keifer served as Speaker of the House of Representatives from 1881 to 1883. (loc)

*   *   *

In the early morning on April 2, Colonel Keifer formed his Third Division brigade on the other side of the ravine from the Vermonters. "Much difficulty was experienced in getting the troops formed, in consequence of the deep darkness and the deep swamp to be passed through," he reported. He instructed the 6th Maryland at the center of his front line to enter the Confederate works through a sally port discovered in the previous week.

"Our spies had reported an opening in their works . . . perhaps 12 to 20 feet wide," recalled a Maryland lieutenant. "Our orders were to march rapidly to the works in front of us, not to fire a gun, but with fixed bayonets and with a wild rush, and the old accustomed yell, charge right over their strong works." Once through the sally port, the regiment would split to the right and left to clear the way for the rest of the brigade. Two Ohio regiments flanked the Marylanders in the front rank while the rest of Keifer's command formed behind them in two succeeding waves.

Seymour's division attacked along the middle branch of Arthur's Swamp. (ea)

As Sgt. Francis Cordrey tried delivering words of encouragement to his company, the signal gun at Fort Fisher interrupted with what he believed to be "the death knell of every man." The Ohioan started forward and shouted for the men to come along. "After which there was no organization by company or otherwise," he admitted, "it was every man tear through the abatis and kill as many rebels as he could on his own plan."

The oversized 9th New York Heavy Artillery formed the entire second line that quickly ground to a halt as they came under fire. "The shells from the enemy's forts screech over our heads, streaks of seething fire," recalled an officer. "As we get nearer, like a tempest grape and canister plunge, patter and bound around us in all directions. Behind every stump lie one, two or three men very affectionately hugging mother earth as if by close application they were deriving the milk of life." The officer swore at his men and struck them with the flat of his sword. Confederate artillery had the position zeroed in and would destroy the entire lot as long as they cowered in place.

Part of the brigade veered along the branch of Arthur's Swamp that led just in front of the Hart house. Meanwhile, a small party in the 6th Maryland followed Major Clifton K. Prentiss along Keifer's designated path. Upon reaching the wall, the men balked as Prentiss fell with a hideous wound in his chest. But Sgt. John E. Buffington sprang forward, the first man from the division to enter the works, and the assault continued onward.

Colonel Keifer reported that his pioneers dragged

the abatis into the ditch to help the attackers cross the moat. Elsewhere the soldiers thrust their bayonets into the wall to carve out handholds as they scrambled for the top. "Men made ladders of themselves by standing one upon another, thus enabling their comrades to gain the parapets," recalled the Ohio commander.

By the time the first wave followed their assignment and cleared the Confederate works, the frustrated New York officer arrived with his men: "Like a lot of sheep, over a stone wall, we go into the enemy's works."

Erson's two regiments at the Hart house successfully held back the Union attackers in their front. Soon more of Keifer's brigade poured through the earthworks on their left, however, and swung down unexpectedly on the flank of the North Carolinians. "I had seen them, but thought it was our own men," described a Confederate private who learned of his error when a Union officer whacked him over the head twice with his sword. "Before I realized my situation his men were right at his heels with fixed bayonets."

A handful of Confederates held out until all hope passed. "I looked around and saw that there was no one there except myself and the Yankees," recalled a sergeant.

Clifton Kennedy Prentiss and his brother William, a Confederate soldier in Heth's Division, were both wounded on April 2. Many popular accounts describe their reunion in the hospital before both died from their wounds later in the year. (php)

I might not have known that they were there had they not been yelling and shooting at the boys who ran before I did. Well, I felt very light and was anxious to see how fast I could run, so I set out for a foot race and when I quit running, I looked back and could not see a Yankee any where. I know I ran fast, for the balls they shot at me, never overtook me and as I passed the ones they shot before I started, I could hear them whistling through the air; Richmond and Petersburg were both gone and so was I, and I kept going.

The triumphant Union soldiers enjoyed the chaos in the Confederate lines. "Then was when we had the most fun seeing the Rebs throw down their guns or run one way or another to get away," recalled a New Yorker. As a North Carolina musician on the run looked back and found discouragement in the "long blue line, sparkling with flashes of musketry" that rapidly drove "our men in pitifully small numbers in full retreat."

* * *

The sun finally rose as the VI Corps soldiers firmly established their grip on the Confederate earthworks. It warmly shone on their victory in a moment they remembered for the rest of their lives. "Then, and there, the long tried and ever faithful soldiers of the Republic saw daylight!" wrote a Connecticut officer in Wheaton's

These well-preserved earthworks likely mark the spot where the 6th Maryland reached the Confederate line. (ea)

division. "Such a shout as tore the concave of that morning sky, it were worth dying to hear."

Sergeant Francis Cordrey of the 126th Ohio in Seymour's division was still inspired years later when he wrote his memoirs:

> At this stage of the battle, the light of day begin to dawn, not only the light of the rising sun in the east, but the light of the rising sun of justice, freedom and liberty, that shall forever shine on every American citizen. Yes, we trust it was the dawning of a new day that shall know no more rebels in our land, no North, no East, no South and no West, and shall know but one flag and that flag the stars and stripes.

Private Perry of Getty's division agreed that it was the grandest sight he ever saw. "The flags all seemed to have more and new luster and the stars seem to be brighter and new glory added to the stripes," he later glowed. "Old Glory appeared to be a living thing. Who would not die for this flag? Thousands have done it before and more to follow."

Sergeant Milton Blickensderfer, 126th Ohio, received the Medal of Honor for his capture of a Confederate flag. (php)

Despite their excitement, a truly decisive victory demanded further action. The VI Corps' hard work was not yet done for the day, but rallying the men to move on to their secondary objectives proved a challenge. "Though thus far the assault had been crowned with success, the greatest danger was still before us," recalled Colonel Keifer, who remembered the swift counterattack that doomed Gordon's assault at Fort Stedman a week before.

"It was most difficult to keep the line formed," recalled a Vermont lieutenant. "The troops in their enthusiasm would break away in bodies of from ten to fifty, heedless of commands, charging this point or that, wherever the enemy attempted to make a stand."

"Here and there, an all directions, over the vast

plain, the Union flag was waving, with only a score of men to guard it in many instances, all were rushing forward," wrote a Wisconsin officer.

This Currier & Ives lithograph provides a hackneyed attempt to depict the April 2 fighting around Petersburg. (loc)

We formed one grand skirmish wave, which nothing could check; the enemy was retiring. Aide-de-camps were galloping about endeavoring to drive us back, that the battalions might reform. We knew nothing of the designs of Grant, nor of the extent of our victory as a whole. I was imbued with the idea that the South Side Railroad should be torn up; and, with the regimental colours and about twenty men, I pressed forward to accomplish the task.

Not every elated member of the VI Corps focused on military targets. As Private Perry traveled with a few of his Pennsylvania comrades along the Boydton Plank Road they interacted with a few local residents. "Meet a number of people going to church both old and young," he chronicled in his diary. "Meet a number of young girls from 16 to 20 at a Rebel sutler's shop, treated them to apple jack and had considerable amount of sport. They were smart and sincere pure Rebels and full of fume." Eventually, an adjutant rode up and admonished the young troublemakers to return to their unit now making their way for the railroad.

With the Union attackers disoriented by their success, a swift counterattack could potentially take advantage of their lost cohesiveness. But at the moment, only two gray-clad riders galloped down from Petersburg.

The Death of A.P. Hill

CHAPTER TEN

Lieutenant General Ambrose Powell Hill suffered severely throughout the winter from the debilitating sickness that frequently rendered him useless the previous year. On March 20, he had finally relented to a temporarily sick leave and recuperated at his uncle's home in Chesterfield County. On March 29, he accompanied his uncle to the Confederate capital, where speculation rang wild of its possible evacuation. This greatly annoyed the general, who then declared he did not wish to survive the fall of Richmond.

In just a few days' time, he found opportunity to back up his words.

Hill returned from his furlough to command the Third Corps on March 31. The 39-year-old Virginia native kept his headquarters on the western outskirts of Petersburg at the Widow Knight's house, Indiana. As he recovered, the general stayed across the street at the Venable cottage, joined by his wife and two young children.

Woken to the news of the IX Corps assault east of Petersburg along the Jerusalem Plank Road, Hill quickly dressed and asked for an update from Heth or Wilcox. At this time, however, word of the Union assault to the southwest had not yet reached the inner lines. Hill determined to meet with Robert E. Lee at the commander's headquarters at Edge Hill, one and a half miles away on Cox Road. He quickly rode west accompanied by three staff officers.

Along the way, Hill was alerted to his broken lines. Upon reaching Edge Hill, he immediately ordered one of his party to return to his headquarters and inform Col. William H. Palmer, Third Corps chief of staff, to follow to the right and assist in rallying the men. As the

A small granite marker denotes the spot where A.P. Hill fell. (ea)

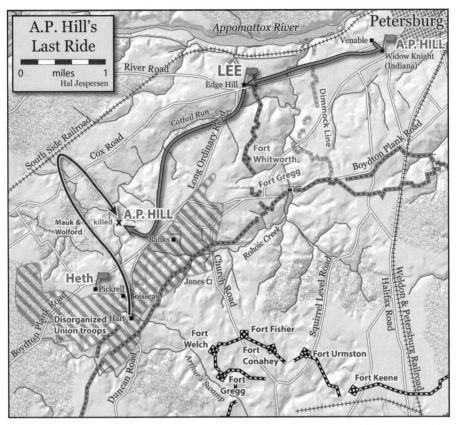

A. P. HILL'S LAST RIDE—Hill's judgment and mindset during his April 2 ride open room for speculation. His declining health, suffering reputation, and earlier claims that he did not want to survive the fall of Richmond have led some to believe that he may have been on a brash suicide ride for redemption—though there is no primary anecdotal evidence.

courier galloped away to deliver the first news of the breakthrough, Hill climbed off his horse to meet inside with Lee. Lieutenant General James Longstreet—weary from his overnight journey south from Richmond—napped in an adjacent room as the two generals talked. He soon roused to discuss positioning his reinforcements.

After learning of the April 1 disaster to the west, Lee had instructed Longstreet to transfer a division down to Petersburg. Longstreet ordered Maj. Gen. Charles W. Field to board his five brigades on train cars and hurry to the front, but the first of their arrivals could not be expected until noon at the earliest.

A few minutes later, Col. Charles S. Venable of Lee's staff rushed into the house with exciting news. He encountered a wounded officer on crutches hobbling back from the temporarily invalid quarters at Mahone's former winter camp. The retreating convalescent reported that enemy skirmishers had driven them out

In November 1864, Robert E. Lee established his headquarters to the Turnbull House at Edge Hill. (cf)

and presently lurked just half a mile south of Lee's headquarters. Venable also observed "wagons and teamsters dashing rather wildly down the River Road in the direction of Petersburg."

Lee ordered Venable to determine the severity of the situation. Hill leaped up and followed the staff officer, accompanied by Sgt. George W. Tucker and Pvt. William H. Jenkins as an escort. As the quartet rode south, they lingered at Cattail Run to water their horses. "While thus engaged the enemy made his presence known by firing on us some straggling shots from the direction of the huts and hill towards the Boydton plank road," recalled Venable. Alarmed by the danger, the officer secured a handful of skirmishers to advance in front of the riders to make some show of force.

Hill quickly grew tired of the slower pace of their infantry escort and spurred his horse forward. Venable realized the general's sole intent "was to reach his troops at all hazards."

As the party sped forward, they came upon two Union soldiers who strayed too far from their regiment. Tucker and Jenkins instantly rode in front of A. P. Hill and demanded that the Federals surrender. The surprised Yankees complied. "Jenkins, take them to General Lee," ordered Hill, and the three riders continued onward, barely skirting the invalid cabins now evidently full of Yankees.

Mahone's Division, often times the offensive sparkplug during the campaign, camped near Edge Hill during the winter. (hw)

Tucker began to worry about the general's noticeably erratic behavior and called out, "Please excuse me, General, but where are you going?"

"Sergeant, I must go to the right as quickly as possible," Hill replied, pointing southwest along Cattail Run to where Henry Heth made his headquarters three miles away at the Pickrell house. "We will go up this side of the branch to the woods, which will cover us until reaching the field in rear of General Heth's quarters. I hope to find the road clear."

Noticing some Confederate artillery along Cox Road, Hill dispatched Colonel Venable to position the batteries in defense of Lee's headquarters. "From that time on I kept slightly ahead of the General," recalled Tucker, now the lone bodyguard for the Third Corps commander. "I had my pistol drawn since the affair of the Federal stragglers."

The pair continued their journey along Cattail Run and stayed in the woods until they reached an open field opposite the Harman house on Boydton Plank Road, less than half a mile from their destination at the Pickrell house. As they rode, Hill ordered his companion, "Sergeant, should anything happen to me you must go back to General Lee and report it."

Tucker advanced ahead into the clearing and kept on the right. He believed the two could find safe shelter in a small swampy forest just past the open ground. As the sergeant drew near the edge of the field, he noticed a handful of large oak trees at the wood line. A small group of Union soldiers rested about 50 yards past the oaks boiling coffee while oblivious to their distinguished guests.

At the same time, a pair of Union soldiers from the 138th Pennsylvania returned from an unofficial expedition to the South Side Railroad and hungrily wandered through the swamp towards the breakfast.

Ambrose Powell Hill commanded the Third Corps since the summer of 1863. Well acclaimed as an effective infantry commander in the first half of the war, recurring illness prevented "Little Powell" from matching those expectations following his elevation to corps command. (loc)

*   *   *

Corporal John W. Mauk and Pvt. Daniel Wolford had participated in the morning charge with Keifer's brigade of the Third Division. After gaining the Confederate earthworks, a portion of the brigade— including Mauk and Wolford—separated from the corps and pushed forward for the railroad. Crossing the Boydton Plank Road, the pair spotted a wagon train and fruitlessly chased after the prize. The duo continued on for the railroad and found some crowbars in a sawmill next to the tracks, which they used to tear up several rails. After this destruction, the two Pennsylvanians took the quickest route along a corduroy road through the woods to rejoin their comrades.

As they approached, Mauk noticed the Confederate officers immediately: "We had just entered the swamp, when they advanced with cocked revolvers in their hands, which were leveled at us. Seeing a large oak tree close to the road, we took it for protection against any movement they would be likely to make."

The pair positioned themselves on the same side of the oak and poked their rifles out, one on top of the

LEFT: Bryan Grimes oversaw the stubborn Confederate defense at Fort Mahone which held the IX Corps in check for the duration of the day. RIGHT: The only officer General Lee addressed by name, Henry Heth oversaw operations west of Hatcher's Run on April 2. (loc)(loc)

other. Mauk's aimed his barrel for Hill while Wolford shakily pointed his at Tucker.

Hill, defiantly closing his horse within 20 yards of the Pennsylvanians, declared, "We must take them."

"If you fire, you'll be swept to hell!" cried out Tucker. Wolford consented that the jig was up and lowered his rifle with the riders only 10 yards away. Mauk refused to surrender in the hour of victory. "I could not see it," he recalled—and directed to the private: "Let us shoot them."

Wolford snapped his rifle back up as he fired and missed his target altogether, but Mauk's bullet found its mark. Hill crumpled out of the saddle to the ground with a fatal wound through the heart.

Startled by the experience, the two Union soldiers hurried to join their comrades preparing coffee and left the lifeless body on the ground.

Tucker, meanwhile—observing no movement in the general—yanked Champ's bridle and rushed away atop his own horse. Soon, he switched horses to the faster Champ and raced back to Edge Hill headquarters by the most direct route, taking little regard for his own personal safety. Just before reaching the Turnbull house, he encountered Colonel Palmer, and the pair rode on to meet with General Lee. They found him already dressed and mounted in front of his headquarters. The sergeant reported Hill's last order and informed Lee of the general's demise.

The Confederate commander's eyes brimmed with tears as he listened to the details of the encounter. He then directed Palmer and Tucker to the Venable cottage to inform Mrs. Hill of her husband's death. "Colonel," Lee advised, "break the news to her as gently as possible."

Hill's headquarters guard, the Fifth Alabama Battalion, devised a way to retrieve their general's body. Half a dozen procured Union uniforms and pretended to escort a handful of the unit still in their Confederate jackets to the south as prisoners. They encountered

Present at the firing on Fort Sumter, Charles Scott Venable taught mathematics at the University of Virginia after the war. (uva)

The SCV monument to A. P. Hill curiously identifies the general being killed by a "band of stragglers." (ea)

Mauk, still breakfasting near the swamp, and inquired if anyone had been killed nearby.

The corporal bought the ruse and directed the Alabamians to the undisturbed body, which still lay warm. Only after he later reported his tale at the VI Corps headquarters was he informed: "You have killed General A.P. Hill."

Along A. P. Hill's Last Ride

The Venable and Widow Knight houses no longer exist. Their location today is near where U.S. Route 1 crosses the modern CSX Railroad near Atlantic Street.

Most of the general's final ride spans across private property. The three different markers designating the death of A. P. Hill can be confusing to visitors. Keeping with a tendency to place memorials where they are easily accessible along highways, the Sons of Confederate Veterans erected a granite marker around 1914 inscribed to the memory of the general at the northeast intersection of U.S. Route 1 and the Boydton Plank Road.

In 1929, the Virginia Conservation & Development Commission placed one of their gray and black signs found frequently throughout the state across the road to designate "Where Hill Fell."

The actual location is farther in from the highway. To reach the spot where Hill, Tucker, Mauk, and Wolford had their standoff, a visitor can turn in to the Sentry Woods subdivision off Route 1 and circle around to the far end of the neighborhood. A short walking trail leads to a small granite monument marking the true "Spot Where A.P. Hill Was Killed." This ground is preserved by the Civil War Trust.

The general is buried under his monument in Richmond at the corner of Hermitage Road and Labernum Avenue.

Initially buried in Chesterfield County, Hill's remains were transferred to Hollywood Cemetery in 1867 before the general was finally interred in 1892 beneath his monument on Richmond's north side. (ea)

A. P. Hill monument
and burial site
GPS: N 37.58415 W 77.46252

A. P. Hill Sons of Confederate
Veterans monument
GPS: N 37.18947 W 77.47559

A. P. Hill death site
GPS: N 37.19233 W 77.48036

The Sweep to Hatcher's Run

CHAPTER ELEVEN

The VI Corps temporarily lost focus after the initial success in breaking A. P. Hill's lines near Tudor Hall. Small parties plundered the Confederate camps and ventured independently for the railroad. Wright finally gathered back Getty and Wheaton's men close to where they first came over the Confederate works. He formed them perpendicular to this line and set off to assist Seymour's men to the south who were taking on three brigades from Heth's Division.

First in the path of the VI Corps stood Brig. Gen. William McComb's Tennessee Brigade, which had begun the morning beyond the southernmost branch of Arthur's Swamp near Fort Davis. "About four hundred yards south of MacRae's headquarters the works crossed a ready swamp and a little creek that was impassable at all places to the front or rear of our line for many hundred yards," described Tennessee Capt. William H. Harder. "We had cut green pine bushes and created a moat and bridge across this creek at the works, about thirty feet wide."

Davis's Brigade of Mississippians, under temporary command of Col. Andrew M. Nelson, manned the fortifications below McComb while Brig. Gen. John R. Cooke extended the line down to Hatcher's Run. His five North Carolina regiments split themselves along both banks of the stream. Cooke took immediate command of this Confederate force that numbered approximately 1,600—a mere speed bump on the VI Corps' path.

Major General Truman Seymour's division was the first to encounter these Confederates. Truex's brigade had crossed over the earthworks near the six-gun battery along Duncan Road during the breakthrough. The

Pamplin rangers constructed a trail in October 2014 for the Civil War Trust that leads down to their preserved property along Hatcher's Run. (ea)

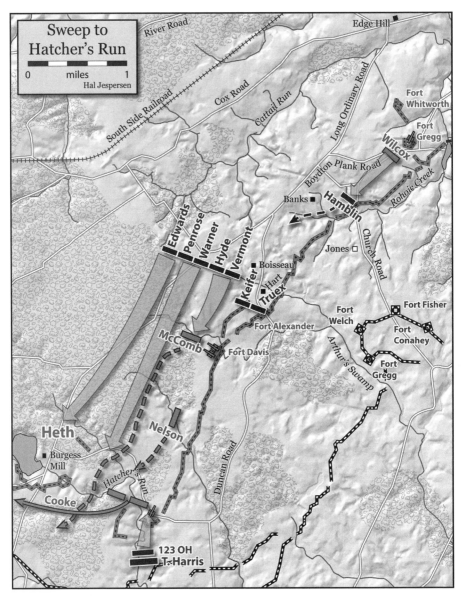

SWEEP TO HATCHER'S RUN—While Wright swung south to Hatcher's Run, Ord's three divisions remained mostly unengaged. A quicker strike to the north could have prevented the problems that would trouble the Union infantry that afternoon.

colonel instantly sent two regiments to the left at the double quick to expand his hold while he remained back at the works to direct the rest of his command to follow.

The brigade quickly ran into Purcell Battery's at Fort Alexander. Captain Lemuel Abbott wrote that the 10th Vermont "sprang into the fort, clubbed and knocked down with their discharged muskets the few remaining men who had not fled or been killed." Some of the Richmond artillerists, "when lying on their backs," seized the lanyards within their reach and "persistently endeavored to fire the pieces." The Vermonters prevented this by "standing dramatically over the prostrate men with inverted guns and fixed bayonet ready to impale them if they persisted."

Their supports had an easier time. "We got in rear of the forts and mowed the Johnies down like grass," claimed Pvt. Simon B. Cummins. "The Johns was panic stricken and run like sheep. They said they well knew what was coming when we began to howl." McComb's Brigade noticed this fighting to their left by "the shouts of the Federals and the yell of the Confederates."

Located on private property, **Fort Alexander still stands impressively strong.** (ea)

Two guns in the fort contested Truex's men as they attempted to negotiate Pole Bridge and press on to Fort Davis. "Our lines became very much scattered and broken," admitted a New Yorker as they hurried down the hill into the swamp. "They moved forward with a terrible loss of men, under our fire across the break on the little bridge in a fast run," remembered Captain Harder. The Confederates ran two field pieces out of Fort Davis to sweep the space between the forts "carrying death across the bridge."

The Union soldiers plunged into the marsh to avoid the fire on the bridge. Despite the water rising in places nearly to their shoulders, they pressed on "with colors flying" and "amid showers of grape and canister" to reach the ditch. After a brief stop that allowed a detachment to move to the winter quarters behind the work to gain a crossfire, the Union party successfully stormed Fort Davis.

McComb determined the fortification's "quick recapture was imperative" and took his remaining regiments out of the earthworks and prepared them for a counterattack. "They poured a steady flame on us as we ran to them and it seemed that we would be exterminated," recalled Captain Harder as the Tennessee soldiers pressed back toward Fort Davis. "We neared their front, they slowed, my men yelled, we closed, one bright flash, a dreadful crash, and before I could think the butt of the guns were carrying everything."

A soldier under William Snyder Truex wrote: "Our boys seem to think that unless Colonel is with them, the machine won't work." (php)

Born in Pennsylvania, William McComb moved to Tennessee in 1854 and commanded a brigade of that state's troops in the war. (loc)

The works were gained "in a regular devils' picnic." Soon, the rest of McComb's Brigade followed into Fort Davis, where the general realigned them in expectation of another Union assault. Colonel Keifer's brigade had arrived at Fort Alexander from the Hart farm.

"Where in the – is 9th New York?" barked out a Union officer. Soon these experienced artillerists were rushed into the fort to man the captured Confederate pieces. "They hurriedly stacked arms, flew to the guns, and, like old veterans, were soon pouring shot and shell," remembered an Ohioan.

"I helped work one of the captured pieces," a corporal later bragged to his parents. "We were in the hardest of the fight before you were out of your beds." Their fire now swept the space between the two forts and forced the Tennesseans back to cover. "The shells howled by me as fast as they could fire their pieces," remembered Harder.

McComb held the Fort Davis position for 20 minutes. His men found protection inside the fort and along a traverse beside the bridge. Eventually they piled logs as best they could to find cover from the barrage. Some members of the 2nd Maryland Battalion, attached to McComb's Brigade, also had previous artillery training. They turned the guns in Fort Davis on the New Yorkers, but their efforts proved to be in vain.

During the fighting between McComb and Seymour, Wright had wheeled five more Union brigades to the south. Getty's three brigades soon formed to the right of Truex and Seymour, with Penrose and Edwards' brigades stretching on to the Boydton Plank Road. Only one Union brigade—Hamblin's—faced to the north with a few batteries to stem any potential counterattacks from Petersburg.

Faced with this overwhelming force, Cooke ordered McComb to withdraw toward Hatcher's Run and made arrangements for the other two Confederate brigades to safely escape. As McComb's men retreated, the Union heavy artillerymen in Fort Alexander reverted back to infantry and charged across Pole Bridge in pursuit.

They briefly halted in Fort Davis and witnessed the effects of their bombardment: "One of their guns was

This view shows the continuation of the Confederates lines from Fort Alexander before they head down the swamp in front of Fort Davis. (ea)

found to be capsized and the carriage broken. By the other gun lay its gunner with half of his head blown off, and nearby, another with his thigh smashed, also a rebel officer who had bitten the dust."

The Tennessee soldiers were not content to abandon their position without a contest and fought their way back through their winter cabins. As they retreated from house to house, Sergeant Manson noticed that a Union soldier "brought his gun to bear on my face at a point blank range of less than forty steps." Manson ducked behind the corner of a hut and "the bark spattered in my face as the ball grazed the log." The sergeant gave "a prayer for the soul of the bravest Yankee I ever saw" and aimed his rifle at the Union soldier's breast. "At the crack of the gun he fell from the earth-works." Manson was struck a few minutes later in the leg and captured as McComb's Brigade fell back under close pursuit.

As Getty's three Union brigades joined the fray, Sgt. Lester G. Hack of the 5th Vermont noticed a squad of the 23rd Tennessee rallying on the colors behind Fort Davis. "I am going after that flag," he declared and took off alone, managing to creep undetected upon their flank.

Reaching the party, he called for the flag, but its bearer refused. Hack swung at the Southerner with his fist and knocked him down. He grabbed the flag and waved his empty musket at the group, ordering them to surrender. While some took flight, Hack surprised his comrades by returning to their lines with 13 prisoners and the Confederate colors tied around his waist.

Under this relentless pressure, many Confederates threw down their guns and surrendered. "The 6th Corps held the road to Petersburg. . . . The works on the run were taken, escape westward was cut off," realized a Maryland soldier who found the situation hopeless. McComb's Brigade was gobbled up, most of them sent to the rear as prisoners.

"The men who captured us belonged to the 138th Pennsylvania, and treated us very kindly, offering us crackers and cheese, which we did not accept," recalled a Confederate. "We were taken back to the rear, to Fort Fisher, where, much to my surprise, we found nearly the whole of our brigade."

Sergeant Manson was taken to a Union field hospital where he saw doctors feverishly amputating limbs to keep up with their building workload. "With a shudder I heard the litter-bearers say, 'Your time next,'" Mason recalled. "I was placed on the table, chloroform was administered, and when I awoke from slumber, my dancing days were over and I was a hopeless cripple for life."

While recovering, he was surprised to see the man

"I can give my foot for such a cause with goodwill," wrote James Marsh Read about his wounding at Fort Davis before dying several days after his amputation. (vt.hs)

John Rogers Cooke joined the Confederate army in 1861 while his father Phillip commanded Union cavalry. (lv)

Lester Goodel Hack recalled the Confederates "were fleeing helter skelter in all directions" when he went after the flag that earned him the Medal of Honor. (php)

he had shot on the works. The wounded Pennsylvanian told his side of the story: "I shot at a feller at the corner of a cabin, and missed him, when he shot me in the breast here, the ball hitting in front on the collarbone and knocking me off the works."

Manson claimed that the two waited on each other for three days, "but that was long enough for God to teach two erring mortals that brave men bore no malice, and as they grasped each other's hand for a final separation, they each breathed a sigh of thankfulness that 'I didn't kill you.'"

* * *

The VI Corps' onslaught next careened into the Mississippians. Major Alfred M. O'Neal, commanding the 1st Confederate Battalion of sharpshooters, made a brief stand and managed to recapture one of their "mud forts." Remnants from the 2nd Maryland rallied beside O'Neal and helped keep Seymour's men temporarily in check, even though it seemed "that the whole Federal Army had been let loose."

Heth advised Colonel Nelson to "get out if he could." But the swift advance of the VI Corps cut off the majority of the Mississippians before they received the orders to retreat. As losses began to pile up, the officers determined to surrender. About 50 swam across Hatcher's Run to escape, one finding a floating log to carry him. O'Neal was badly wounded and captured with the rest of the command.

Lieutenant Franklin L. Hope tore the 11th Mississippi's flag into shreds, tied them to the staff, and threw it into Hatcher's Run to avoid capture. Meanwhile the 2nd Mississippi's flag bearer tore the colors from the staff, "concealed it beneath his little gray jacket," and carried it through his prison experience at Fort Delaware.

The Tennessee soldiers who had also skirmished their way back toward Hatcher's Run found the Union army in control of the bridge at Burgess's Mill. Like the Mississippians they had no choice but to swim to safety. McComb claimed that "there was not the least confusion," and 400 of his command managed to cross.

An enlisted man saw things different. "Soon, we were face to face with a new peril. Our soldiers had dammed up a creek in order to protect our position, and the water backed up some distance. . . . Across this lake we had to go to keep from being captured. We waded in, and soon I saw it was going to be over our heads, for I saw one man drowning in front of me. He stepped in over his head, and his cartridge box and haversack being so heavy; he was carried right under."

Eventually the Tennesseans found a few large downed trees to cross upon.

* * *

Grant had originally planned for Ord's three divisions from the Army of the James near Hatcher's Run to also attack on the morning on April 2. But as the XXIV Corps massed for an attack on the earthworks, Ord deemed a charge impractical. "The ground here was so difficult to move over, being covered with brush and scrub timber, and so spongy from recent rains that it would not bear a horse," reported an engineer. Furthermore, a Union officer found the earthworks "protected by deep and wide trenches which surrounded it, and which the enemy had flooded with water to further impede our entrance."

Ord expressed his concern to Grant, who responded: "I do not wish you to fight your way over difficult barriers against defended lines." He told the Army of the James commander to keep his men prepared for a frontal assault should his Confederate counterparts show signs of weakening. However, Ord's primary focus for the morning of April 2 revolved around reinforcing the VI Corps if they managed to storm the works.

Around 6:00 a.m., Grant instructed Ord to move to Wright's assistance. Ord sent Foster's division with

Hatcher's Run – "A tortuous stream with gnarled trees with unsightly branches... The banks on either side are hid by impenetrable thickets of bushes and vines." (ea)

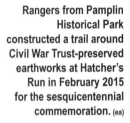

Rangers from Pamplin Historical Park constructed a trail around Civil War Trust-preserved earthworks at Hatcher's Run in February 2015 for the sesquicentennial commemoration. (ea)

Potter's and Curtis's brigades from Brig. Gen. John W. Turner's division. With Heth's Division still firmly in place behind their fortifications, the five Northern brigades marched back through their own lines before they reached the VI Corps' battlefield. Birney's three brigades of United States Colored Troops remained at Hatcher's Run, as did Brig. Gen. Thomas M. Harris's three West Virginia regiments. The 123rd Ohio, of Potter's brigade, remained in place on the picket line opposite Cooke's North Carolinians.

The Confederate brigade began the morning straddling Hatcher's Run in strong entrenchments. "Our position in the fort was only tenable, provided the troops on our left held their position," realized a North Carolinian. "Consequently, the issue of the fight was awaited by us with much anxiety."

"Our feelings would rise or fall in proportions as we would hear the Confederate 'yell' or the Yankee 'huzza,'" recalled a member of the brigade. "After a while the 'huzza' seemed to prevail." Soon a courier dashed into the fort and informed the men that the lines were broken.

Just as Cooke's men began to retreat toward Burgess's Mill, Turner instructed Harris to advance a strong skirmish line across Hatcher's Run to determine if the Confederates had abandoned their works. "We were not to be denied admittance to their inner circle much longer," recalled a West Virginia captain who claimed to not balk at the obstructions the North Carolinians had placed in the stream. The bluecoats "plunged right in" and found the debris in the water useful. "By holding to the limbs a number of the foremost men scrambled across without getting wet."

The obstacles did, however, buy time for Cooke's men to evacuate. Harris reported that the majority of the defenders successfully retreated "whilst my men were

Edward Otho Cresap Ord is pictured here with the table used by Lee in the McLean House at Appomattox. Ord took the table with him after the surrender. (loc)

struggling through a very dense difficult slashing in front of these works." The North Carolinians moved west for White Oak Road before following Claiborne Road up to Sutherland Station on the South Side Railroad.

Those who remained offered no resistance. At almost no cost, the XXIV Corps captured several hundred prisoners, two brass Napoleons, and two flags. Among their bounty was the flag of the 2nd Maryland, whose bearer had begun the morning several miles to the north up near Fort Davis.

Thomas Maley Harris served as a physician in present day West Virginia before the war. (loc)

Forts Gregg and Whitworth

CHAPTER TWELVE

After the blue wave crashed over the sparse Confederate defenses down to Hatcher's Run, Wright linked up with Ord's men near Burgess Mill. The VI Corps' move to the south bought Robert E. Lee a little time to scrape together a patchwork line to slow the federal advance on Petersburg.

The loss of his Third Corps commander still lingered in Lee's mind. "He is at rest now, but we who are left are the ones to suffer," the gray general in chief declared, recognizing that he could not take any more time to mourn Hill's death. The VI Corps breakthrough seriously threatened the continued existence of the Army of Northern Virginia.

The fall of Maj. Gen. Cadmus M. Wilcox's line cut Lee's communications with a large portion of his army. The strength and position of the Confederates driven from Five Forks still remained a mystery, as did the fate of most of Heth's Division, which was now also separated. Around the Turnbull house, Lee could only rely on the handful of artillery units detailed by General Hill to guard Cox Road to protect his headquarters. Longstreet still did not expect his infantry reinforcements until the early afternoon.

At 10:00 a.m., Lee wired the capital: "I see no prospect of doing more than holding our position here till night. I am not certain that I can do that. If I can I shall withdraw tonight north of the Appomattox, and, if possible, it will be better to withdraw the whole line tonight from the James River. . . . I advise that all preparation be made for leaving Richmond tonight." With the order issued to abandon both Petersburg and Richmond, Lee still needed to buy time for as organized a withdrawal as possible.

Said one soldier who was at Fort Gregg: "Never have I witnessed anything to compare with that bloody struggle for its possession on the one side and retention on the other. . . . The flags alternated, carrying with them in their rise and fall the hopes and fears of the thousands of overwrought onlookers." (ea)

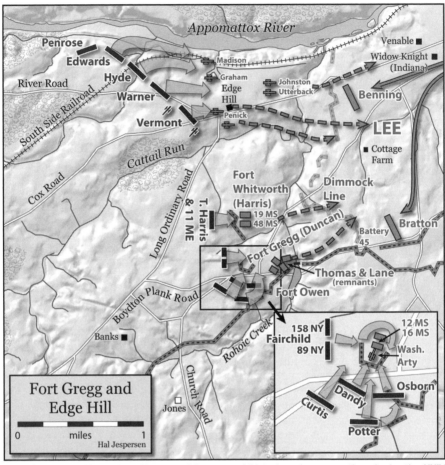

FORT GREGG AND EDGE HILL—Many participants and historians have questioned why the XXIV Corps fixated so strongly on the Confederate stronghold at Fort Gregg, which easily could have been bypassed. However, their frantic charges—along with those of the VI Corps against Lee's artillery—demonstrate Grant's determination to maintain the initiative that characterizes his success in the final weeks of the war in Virginia.

As Lee delivered the devastating update to the capital, Wilcox hoped to seize the initiative and reclaim part of his lines. He organized a motley force from 600 refugees of Lane's and Thomas's brigades. This group swiftly pushed back a small Union scouting party from Hamblin's brigade who attempted to expand the break farther up the Boydton Plank Road past the Banks house. Lane then temporarily formed the remnant of his brigade into a makeshift line along Church Road at a right angle to their original position that morning.

In the meantime, Lee received an enraging response from his suggestion to immediately evacuate Richmond. "To move tonight will involve the loss of many valuables, both for the want of time to pack and of transportation" scolded President Davis, who fostered a lingering faith that the army could restore their defenses. Lee reportedly ripped the telegram to shreds and adamantly restated the situation: "I think it is absolutely necessary that we should abandon our position tonight. I have given all the necessary orders on the subject to the troops, and the operation, though difficult, I hope will be performed successfully."

*   *   *

As the VI Corps turned back from Hatcher's Run, joined now by Gibbon's XXIV Corps, only two small earthen fortifications stood between them and Petersburg's inner lines—Forts Gregg and Whitworth. Erected in the fall of 1864, they offered the only hope for the Confederates to slow their Union pursuers long enough for reinforcements to appear on the railroad from Richmond to temporarily provide Petersburg salvation.

Jefferson Davis was attending service in St. Paul's Church when informed of the capture of Petersburg's outer defenses. (na)

Colonel Thomas O. Osborn led the vanguard of the XXIV Corps as they marched up the Boydton Plank Road after clearing out the Hatcher's Run line. At 8:30 a.m., his brigade arrived near the Harmon house and deployed with their right flank anchored on the Confederate fortifications previously captured by the VI Corps.

Wilcox's earlier counterattack had contained Hamblin's brigade from expanding the breech in the lines. Now the major general turned to Brig. Gen. Nathaniel M. Harris, whose Mississippians had just arrived from north of the Appomattox. Wilcox hoped these four regiments from Mahone's Division could buy time for additional reinforcements to fill the unmanned section of the Dimmock Line. "We found everything in confusion; our lines had been ruptured everywhere, and the Union troops were in possession," remembered Pvt. Frank H. Foote upon the Mississippi brigade's arrival.

Cadmus Marcellus Wilcox had faced this kind of adversary before. On May 3, 1863, while Lee was getting the best of Joseph Hooker near Chancellorsville, Wilcox's Alabama Brigade was the only force standing between the VI Corps and the rear of Lee's army. Flush with victory from their dramatically successful storming of Marye's Heights near Fredericksburg, the corps— then under the command of John Sedgwick—found their movement repeatedly delayed by Wilcox's skillful defense in depth. By the time Sedgwick had his men in position to overwhelm the Alabamians, reinforcements from Chancellorsville had arrived in the nick of time to throw back the attack near Salem Church. Now in command of a division, Wilcox hoped to repeat this mastery once more.

One of Harris's men found the major general to be "inclined to be a little profane that morning." As the Mississippians marched past, Wilcox denigrated his own

Cadmus Marcellus Wilcox authored *Rifles and Rifle Practice* as a West Point textbook before the war. (loc)

Stationed in the Washington defenses for much of the war, James Meech Warner was severely wounded in his first engagement at Spotsylvania before promotion to brigade command. (loc)

men, who'd broken, saying each Mississippian was "equal to one hundred of those damned cowardly fellows."

Harris deployed his men on a slight ridge 400 yards in front of Fort Gregg and pulled both his flanks back around the crest in hopes of diminishing his small numbers to his opponent's eye. The portly Mississippian also threw out skirmishers but cautioned them not to be as aggressive as normal. Nearby, Confederate artillery harassed Osborn's steady advance while Harris positioned his brigade.

Meanwhile, the Vermont Brigade led the VI Corps march up Boydton Plank Road on their return from the Hatcher's Run expedition. Wright sought to extend Osborn's line to Cox Road. First, however, he sent Hamblin's brigade—who fended off Wilcox's earlier counterattack—to assist the IX Corps south of Petersburg and placed the two brigades of his Third Division in reserve on their early morning battlefield.

The Vermonters took position on a hill to the left of the road with Warner's brigade on their left. Colonel Hyde deployed his men at a refused angle to Warner, and his line was then extended by Edwards's and Penrose's brigades to the South Side Railroad. They too came under a heavy artillery fire from two batteries of Lt. Col. William T. Poague's Battalion, positioned by A. P. Hill just before he rode to his death. As the infantry shied behind the crest of a ridge along their new line, a Pennsylvania remembered it "was death to rise above it."

At 9:00 a.m., Osborn ordered his brigade to charge. "Stand like iron, my brave boys!" called General Harris as he walked his line. "Stand like iron!" The Union advance steadily drove back the Mississippians' skirmish line and soon gained the shelter of a sunken road 150 yards in front of the main line. The two sides exchanged fire for some time until Harris noticed the Vermonters maneuvering past his flanks, threatening to expose their unsupported position. He ordered his men to slowly pull back toward Forts Gregg and Whitworth. This orderly retreat allowed the Confederates to continue their delaying tactics before bringing on a general engagement but forced Lane to abandon his line along Church Road.

Wilcox's new position stretched west from Battery 45 along Boydton Plank Road in several thin lines. Most of the remnants of Lane's and Thomas's Brigades took position in between Battery 45 and Fort Gregg, though a few found refuge in the fort itself. There they met Lt. Francis McElroy's section of the Washington Artillery of New Orleans. As the Louisianan placed his two three-inch ordnance rifles into position, Harris's 12th and 16th Mississippi marched into the fort. Lieutenant Colonel James H. Duncan took command of the fort and its

300-350 strong garrison. Harris led the other 200 men of his brigade in the 19th and 48th Mississippi into Fort Whitworth, where they joined four rifled guns in the six-sided enclosure. Wilcox felt confident that the artillery in these forts, with their wide fields of fire, could mutually protect one another in the looming assault.

"Men, the salvation of Lee's army is in your keeping," he declared to the ragtag crew of North Carolinians, Georgians, Louisianans, and Mississippians assembled in Fort Gregg. He stated it was their duty to hold the enemy in check for two hours so that Field's Division could arrive and fill the Dimmock Line. One of the garrison's defenders responded: "Tell General Lee that Fort Gregg will never be surrendered."

As the Confederates steeled themselves for the coming assault, they were disgusted to see the four rifled guns pack up and abandon Fort Whitworth. Third Corps Chief of Artillery Reuben Lindsay Walker determined that his pieces should not be lost in the likely fall of this position and ordered them out. He also wanted the two ordnance rifles in Fort Gregg to leave the fort, but by that point, Union skirmishers had already crept within close enough distance to prevent their withdrawal.

The defenders could now only hope that their own resolve and the forts' mutually supportive design could provide their salvation. "[Fort Gregg] was built for the very purpose for which it served, to resist an opposing army in case the main line of works were carried," recalled Pvt. Frank H. Foote of the 48th Mississippi. "A deep moat or ditch surrounded it, which crossed into the gorge by a few feet of earth left intact." Two parapets inside the work, one for infantry and the other for artillery, provided a firing platform that covered the surrounding marshy ground.

A strong zigzag palisade of 20-inch pines loopholed for musketry enclosed the rear of the lunette earthwork. "It had a well-fitted stockade of logs, with portholes 12 feet high for muskets, extending from wing to wing, with a stationary gate in the center," an artilleryman in its garrison remembered. The gunner thought the fortification provided "an impregnable defense against infantry."

Fort Whitworth stood 600 yards north of Fort Gregg. During the winter the Mississippians found its timber supports an easily accessible source for firewood. With a weakened structural integrity, the fort's walls washed partly away by the early 1865 rains, leaving Private Foote to lament that "it did not have the strength of an ordinary rifle pit."

Thomas Ogden Osborn studied law under Lew Wallace before the war. (na)

Nathaniel Harrison Harris's Mississippi Brigade suffered heavy casualties in 1864 and only contained about 500 members in 1865. (mhi)

*   *   *

Gibbon reinforced Osborn with the two other

Harris's Mississippians set fires to their former winter quarters west of Fort Whitworth to slow the Union advance. (ea)

brigades in Brig. Gen. Robert S. Foster's division. Brigadier General John W. Turner also brought his three brigades up in reserve, meaning the Southerners now faced 11 total brigades aiming to storm Petersburg before Longstreet's arrival. Gibbon left his artillery at Hatcher's Run, however, and wanted to find some nearby batteries to assist in the assault before he would move his men forward. The Third Vermont Battery and a section of the First New York State Battery moved forward to a point near Fort Owen and began working their guns on the Confederate forts.

Brigadier General Thomas W. Harris formed his three West Virginia regiments opposite Fort Whitworth near the quarters formerly occupied that winter by the Mississippians. The 11th Maine shifted into position from the right hoping to connect Harris's men, while the rest of Col. George B. Dandy's brigade fronted Fort Gregg. Dandy, in turn, had placed his men to the left of Osborn's brigade in the first wave to storm the Confederate position. Osborn deployed the 62nd Ohio as skirmishers preparatory for the assault.

By 1:00 p.m., everybody was in position.

*   *   *

Colonel Duncan paced the ramparts of Fort Gregg, extolling his men to hold their fire. "Keep down men; keep down!" cried his officers with drawn swords as Osborn's skirmishers crept forward. "The fort was as full of men as ever a dog was of fleas," recalled Pvt. Michael Wetzel as his 39th Illinois formed behind a marshy swamp just 150 yards in front of Gregg. In between their massed lines and the Confederate position, the Boydton Plank Road ran parallel across the entire front.

Osborn's men pushed for the earthwork, clearing the swamp and crossing the road before the Confederates finally unleashed their devastating fire. "Grape were being planted," recalled the Illinois private, "not as farmers plant corn . . . but by the bucket full, perhaps barrel, for two of the men of my company who were killed each had three grapeshot through them."

Just before reaching the ditch, a shot struck Wetzel in the right arm, but the private bounded ahead and claimed to be the first to reach the moat. He tumbled forward for a hard landing into the deep trench that briefly knocked him unconscious. A handful of survivors dove in behind the private for protection.

As the first assault melted away before the walls of Fort Gregg, Private Foote viewed the aftermath of Osborn's attack from Fort Whitworth: "The battlements were wreathed in smoke, and his men went down by the hundreds. The smoke wafted. . . . [W]e could see the ground strewn with many a blue-clad fellow, while the rear was full of fugitives."

The Mississippians could not relax for long before the next wave of Union attackers advanced at the double quick. This time, the garrison opened fire at 300 yards' range. The outnumbered defenders loaded multiple weapons and some designated soldiers continued to reload while those on the front rank rapidly discharged the pieces, exchanging their spent weapons for fresh rifles. The two regiments at Whitworth fired into Foster's flank as their commander shouted, "Give 'em hell, boys!"

More bluecoats dove headlong into the moat to seek shelter from the storm of lead, and a handful continued to press forward, climbing up the fort's walls. "Nothing daunted by the terrific slaughter of their comrades, these brave men swarmed up by clinging to the sides of the ditch and pushing each other up," recalled Foote. "As the first raised themselves to the parapet they were swept away to a man by rapid volleys and rolled back."

Colonel Osborn jumped into the ditch and personally helped boost his soldiers up the wall, shouting, "Men, we must take this fort before the enemy receives reinforcements." As the defenders raised themselves up to the parapet to fire, they had to first use their bayonets to knock away the muzzles of those Union soldiers clinging desperately to the ramparts before discharging their piece into the swarming mass below.

Wetzel awoke to find himself nearly buried by loose dirt kicked down by the men climbing over him. He recognized a member of his company scaling the wall beside him and tugged on his pants leg for help. His comrade stopped to unbury the private and applied a makeshift tourniquet out of Wetzel's own handkerchief

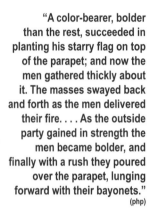

"A color-bearer, bolder than the rest, succeeded in planting his starry flag on top of the parapet; and now the men gathered thickly about it. The masses swayed back and forth as the men delivered their fire. . . . As the outside party gained in strength the men became bolder, and finally with a rush they poured over the parapet, lunging forward with their bayonets."
(php)

to stop the bleeding of his deep wound, though the Illinois soldier eventually lost his arm. He continued to hug Fort Gregg's walls and later recalled that other wounded soldiers were not as fortunate and began to drown in the deep mud: "I could see them struggling in the water from where I lay helpless."

As the Confederates focused their attention on the Union attackers in the ditch, another wave composed of men from Turner's division came rushing on with a loud huzzah. Among Curtis's brigade stood the 23rd Illinois—a mostly immigrant regiment who dubbed themselves the Western Irish Brigade. Many in this unit carried the lever-action 16-shot Henry Rifle, and their impact was immediately noticed. "One fellow I remember especially, who was on his knees, about eight or 10 feet distant from me, working the lever and sending the balls with such rapidity as to cause great havoc and commotion among the Johnnies," remembered a fellow Illinois soldier. "Had all our boys been provided with those deathdealers, the fort would have been taken in much less time."

The defenders spread themselves out to cover every part of the fort's walls and detailed 25 men to guard the palisade gate at the rear. In desperation, a handful of artillerymen considered cutting the fuses of their shells to four or five seconds and throwing them over the fort as makeshift grenades. Others hurled solid-shot cannonballs on the heads of the Union soldiers in the ditch and began tearing away the brick chimneys from the few tents in the fort to provide additional ammo.

"Gregg raged like the crater of a volcano, emitting its flashes of deadly battle fires, enveloped in flame and

cloud, wreathing our flag as well in honor as in the smoke of death," recalled the Mississippi commander at Fort Whitworth. "It was a glorious struggle."

"The little fort was enveloped in a surging mass on assailants," remembered a Maine captain. "They filled the ditches, and eagerly sought for a footway by which to reach the stubborn defenders, who fought with magnificent desperation." Only one footway led into the fort—the incomplete rifle pit extending past the northwest corner once designed to reach Fort Whitworth—and the Confederates swept this face with a constant fire.

Lieutenant George Payne was in command of Dandy's sharpshooter battalion hunkered down near this corner. A veteran of the Mexican War as well as service on the frontier, the 45-year-old called on his men to follow and darted alone up the deadly path. Avoiding the enemy's fire on the ramp, he flung himself headlong into the fort and vigorously swung his saber among the enemy. The rest of the sharpshooters took advantage of his distraction and surged up the ramp and into the fort

Elsewhere, a Union color bearer sought to motivate the mass still cowering in the moat and tossed the national colors over the earthworks, stimulating the men to again scramble their way over the top.

As the Union infantry scaled the works directly in front of the Washington Artillery, they noticed Pvt. Lawrence Berry about to pull the lanyards on one of the guns, double loaded with canister. "Don't fire that gun; drop that lanyard, or we'll shoot!" demanded the Federals.

While Harris's men clung to Fort Gregg, Gordon's Second Corps fought a similarly desperate battle around Fort Mahone to the southwest of Petersburg. (loc)

This 1961 painting by Sydney A. King shows the battle for Fort Gregg: Pvt. Berry about to pull the lanyard while Cpl. Henry M. Day of the 39th Illinois plants the colors on the parapet to his right. (pnb)

"Shoot and be damned!" declared the Louisianan as he discharged the gun, tearing a great swath of destruction through their ranks. The furious Union soldiers around the cannon immediately turned their weapons on the gunner and pierced him full of bullets.

More Federals scaled the walls and locked into hand-to-hand combat with the Confederates. "Plunge, slide or jump down among the brightly polished steel," remembered a Massachusetts soldier grimly. "Foot to foot. No loading and firing now. Bayonet every man." Another remembered it as the most desperate fighting they experienced during the war: "The men used the butts of their guns and bayonets, while our officers were equally busy with their swords. Inch by inch the Johnnies were forced to yield their ground, but it was not until more than half the fort was in our possession before they would surrender."

A few more Confederates were slain after they threw down their arms, a result produced from the sheer intensity of the combat mixed with anger at Berry's decision to fire his cannon.

By 3:00 p.m., after two hours of awful fighting, the last guns fell silent over the blood-stained walls. The defenders had done all they could to slow the Union juggernaut as it slowly rolled toward Petersburg. "I had about eighty rounds of new cartridges; and when I surrendered, my cartridge box was nearly empty," claimed a North Carolinian.

The fall of Fort Gregg left the two regiments in Fort Whitworth in an untenable position. "Every man for himself," declared General Harris, and the Confederates hustled for the inner defenses of Petersburg. Colonel Joseph M. Jayne of the 48th Mississippi—suffering from a leg wound—stayed in the fort with about 70 of his men who surrendered. Meanwhile, Col. Richard W. Phipps of the 19th Mississippi zigzagged his way across the field until a spent bullet nudged him in the back, and the 180-pounder beelined straight for the Dimmock Line.

General Harris soon tired of his jog and bent over to catch his breath. "I'll be damned if I run any more," he declared until a sharp volley geared his legs back into motion. The Mississippians splashed across Rohoic Creek and settled into Petersburg's inner defenses.

The XXIV Corps lost 714 men in the affair, while only 30 of Fort Gregg's defenders walked out on their own power. Private George Washington Benson was among the handful of Confederate prisoners escorted out of Fort Gregg. As he exited the embattled earthwork, he mournfully looked back over the carnage: "O there left some of my brother soldiers, lying there to rise no more, while others were there crying for help, and no one to assist them. . . . I hope that I shall never witness just such a sight again, for the soldiers lay thick, wounded, dying and dead. . . . O what a sight on the Sabbath."

At Fort Gregg

This modern photograph of Fort Gregg shows the artillery embrasures manned on April 2 by only two rifles pieces. (ea)

GPS: N 37.19787 W 77.45059

The National Park Service preserves Fort Gregg as part of its Western Front Unit. Parking for the site is located on 7th Avenue north of Simpson Road. A short walking path leads around and into the now-unenclosed work.

Sadly, recent development is currently transforming the fields charged across by the XXIV Corps into an industrial complex.

The unfinished rifle pit off the northwest corner of the fort that served as a ramp into the garrison still stands as a stark reminder not to begin a task you cannot be bothered to complete.

At Fort Whitworth

GPS: N 37.20255 W 77.45304

Private William R. Baldwin, 19th Mississippi, is likely the guilty contributor to Fort Whitworth's alternate name. (ef)

Following 7th Avenue underneath the Interstate 85 overpass will bring visitors to Fort Whitworth. The severely eroded fortification remains standing today on the grounds of Central State Hospital. The site is accessible off of 7th Avenue, though visitors should be aware that the psychiatric institution occasionally uses the location as a picnic area and for recreation.

Abraham Wood, the first citizen of Dinwiddie County, settled on the property in 1680. In the next century, Robert Ruffin, a member of the House of Burgesses, constructed Mayfield, which still stands as the oldest brick building in the county. Thomas Whitworth acquired the property through marriage in 1833. Though English by birth, he traveled abroad during the War of 1812 to raise money for the United States, earning the honorary title of captain for his effort.

Captain Whitworth acquired nearly 2,000 acres surrounding Mayfield and owned 23 slaves to work the land. Petersburg resident Fletcher Archer, who later commanded the city militia at the battle of Old Men and Young Boys, married Whitworth's niece and stayed at the plantation to help oversee its production in the 1850s.

After the war, the city of Petersburg purchased the structure and its neighboring land in 1882 and transferred it to the state for the construction of the hospital. In 1969, the building was relocated to its current address along U.S. Route One. A decade later, private citizens purchased the structure from the hospital. Today it operates as a bed and breakfast.

Fort Whitworth also appears on maps with the names Fort Alexander and Fort Baldwin. Artillery officer Edward Porter Alexander claimed that Lee's engineers named the spot to honor him, "a compliment of which I am proud." A Mississippi private recalled a member of his brigade named Baldwin broke the rules during their winter encampment in the area and received the punishment of carrying a log on his shoulders while pacing the ramparts of the fort for long hours. The soldiers continued the joke by referring to the location as Battery Baldwin. After the battle, a Maine soldier saw a board stuck up in the fort with the name Baldwin painted on it.

Close to 30,000 Confederate dead from the siege are buried in Petersburg's Blandford Cemetery (top). Poplar Grove National Cemetery (bottom) is the final resting place for approximately 6,000 Union soldiers, including many of the April 2 casualties. (php)(ea)

Grant and Lee Under Fire

CHAPTER THIRTEEN

General Grant spent an anxious night at his Dabney's Mill headquarters before news of Wright's breakthrough relieved his concerns. After Gibbon captured the Hatcher's Run earthworks, Grant rode forward to personally oversee the final attack on Petersburg. The general in chief hoped his presence at the front could swiftly dissolve any challenges arising from a joint offensive between the VI Corps from the Army of the Potomac and the XXIV Corps from the Army of the James.

As he passed the columns on the plank road, the men heartily cheered their general. "He was mounted on a proud-stepping dark charger, dressed with unusual care and never appeared to better advantage," recalled a Vermont captain. "He was a perfect picture of a conquering hero, but seemed all unconscious of it. The artist who could put Grant and his suite on canvas as he appeared then would win renown."

Around 10:45, Grant dismounted near the Banks house to observe the fighting around Fort Gregg. Seated by the base of tree near the home, he began studying dispatches arriving from his scattered commands. A Confederate battery observed the group of officers and directed their fire toward the party, but Grant remained, determined to stay until all the available intelligence reports could catch up to his location.

"As the fire became hotter and hotter, several of the officers, apprehensive for the general's safety, urged him to move to some less conspicuous position," recalled Col. Horace Porter, "but he kept on writing and talking, without the least interruption from the shots falling around him." One of the shots crashed through the

Although he likely did not stay in the house, General Grant spent the night of April 2 on the Banks house propery. (ea)

Nelson Appleton Miles, future Commanding General of the United States Army, drove the remnants of Heth's Division from their defensive position at Sutherland Station in the afternoon on April 2. (loc)

A fellow gunner believed that William Thomas Poague was "amply equipped with both intelligence and valor to have handled an army division with credit to himself and advantage to the service." (php)

Banks house and lodged in the parlor wall. As Grant completed the last of his new directives, he quizzically looked at his concerned officers and remarked, "Well, I they do seem to have the range on us," before sending them off with orders to all parts of the advancing lines.

*   *   *

Despite the mounting losses of troops and ground throughout the morning and early afternoon, General Lee remained determined to hold on to his inner lines through the end of the day. He planned to withdraw from both Petersburg and Richmond under the cloak of darkness and retreat to the southwest along the Richmond & Danville Railroad for a junction with Johnston's army in North Carolina.

With the last available infantry reserves before Longstreet's reinforcements committed to Forts Gregg and Whitworth, Lee could only rely on the arrival of the rest of Lt. Col. William T. Poague's battalion of Third Corps artillery to hold the Union infantry at bay. Still, these cannoneers put up a tremendous show to slow the VI Corps, who swung their line from its position parallel with the River Road to that perpendicular with the Appomattox. If they reached its bank, they would effectively encircle Petersburg on the south side, leaving a handful of bridges across the river to the north as the only possible escape.

Lee's chief of artillery, Brig. Gen. William N. Pendleton, ordered Poague to hold the Turnbull house "to the last moment," instructing him to sacrifice the guns if necessary but to save the men and horses. "Guns were plentiful, men and horses scarce," realized the lieutenant colonel.

The Virginia artilleryman found Capt. Charles F. Johnston's three guns of the Albemarle Artillery and Capt. Addison W. Utterback's Warrenton Battery in rear of Edge Hill, forced to fall back to a spot just in front of Rohoic Creek by the increased pressure of the VI Corps. He spread his remaining three batteries to protect from Lee's headquarters to the river. Captain Nathan Penick's four rifles of the Pittsylvania Artillery guarded the intersection of Cox Road and Long Ordinary Road with Graham's North Carolina Battery, under command of Capt. Arthur B. Williams, to their right. Lieutenant John W. Yeargain placed the Mississippi cannoneers of his Madison Battery just below the South Side Railroad, which ran close to the Appomattox.

The combined impact of these new arrivals immediately took effect on the already exhausted VI Corps as they moved into position to storm the final position. Once more the Vermont Brigade took the lead

on the charge, this time with all six regiments moving in a single line. The First Vermont Heavy Artillery moved directly along Cox Road. To their left ran the Second, Third, Fifth, Sixth, and Fourth Regiments. A lieutenant directing the placement described it as an impossibility "to ride along the line amid that terrible storm of shot and shell."

Warner's brigade extended the line to the north, as did Hyde and Edwards until the Union soldiers came astride the river. Artillery posted on the opposite bank opened a destructive crossfire as the soldiers dove in the mud to find cover. General Getty ordered a charge on the Confederate artillery, but as soon as the Vermonters stepped off they ran into trouble. "The enemy poured in a very heavy fire of shot and shell from a battery on our right, which completely enfiladed our lines, and a perfect hail-storm of canister from a battery of four guns planted in the garden of the Turnbull house," reported a captain.

General Lee watched from the front lawn of his headquarters as the Union infantry approached. "The spectacle was picturesque and striking," claimed a companion. "Across the extensive fields houses set on fire by shell were sending aloft huge clouds of smoke and tongues of flame; at every instant was seen the quick glare of the Federal artillery, firing from every knoll, and in front came on the charging column, moving at a double quick, with burnished gun-barrels and bayonets flashing in the April sunshine."

One of the Union shells struck the Turnbull house, and eventually the structure burned to the ground.

As Lee retreated from Edge Hill, an officer with him recalled: "He turned his head over his right shoulder, his cheeks flushed, and a sudden flash of the eye showed with what reluctance he retired before the fire directed upon him." (php)

The VI Corps contented themselves with the smoldering ruins of Edge Hill as the furthest extent of their advance on April 2. (loc)

Meanwhile, a squad of Pennsylvanians worked their way around the left of Poague's Battalion and opened at a close range, compelling the gunners to abandon their artillery.

The nearby musketry also compelled Lee to leave his headquarters. He slowly rode for the inner line, at last manned by Field's Division. If the Union generals realized Richmond's defenses had been weakened, a direct assault there would doom the Confederate capital. "It has happened as I told them it would at Richmond," Lee commented as he rode, remembering the passive-aggressive complaints he received that morning from his president. "The line has been stretched until it has broken."

Lee's reluctant retreat caught the attention of the Union artillery. Soon a handful of shells struck the ground behind the Confederate party, which enraged the general. No choice remained, however, but to continue his way into the city.

During the engagement at Edge Hill, Colonel Hyde had observed a "fine-looking old officer on a gray horse" directing the movements at the Turnbull house. When he reached the burning structure, he asked a wounded artilleryman who had led the battery. "General Robert E. Lee, sir," the Confederate replied, "and he was the last man to leave these guns."

At the Banks House

Admission to Pamplin Historical Park will grant visitors access to the Banks house grounds. A passcode gate regulates visitation to this satellite property, so please inquire with park staff about viewing Grant's headquarters on April 2, 1865.

This original antebellum structure beside the Banks house served as its kitchen and slave quarters. (ea)

This historically renovated house is one of the oldest in Dinwiddie County, dating back to the 1750s or 1760s. It is an example of a telescoping house—as the owners' wealth and prosperity increased, so too did the home expand over time from the original one-and-a-half-story structure. Scottish immigrant Thomas Banks purchased the house and 331 connected acres in 1839.

Banks called his farm Wakefield and, rather than growing tobacco, operated it as a market farm for the nearby city of Petersburg. He grew oats, wheat, Indian corn, Irish potatoes, and sweet potatoes. The 1840 census shows that he owned 12 slaves. Ten years later, only four remained, all over the age of 40. Pamplin Historical Park preserves one of their original homes next to the house, a rare slave outbuilding still standing in the county.

Thomas Banks died around November 1, 1853, and left his elderly widow Margaret with the property. She was unable to manage the farm and household on her own and arranged with her son John to live in the house and manage the business. John brought along his own

This 1864 Andrew McCallum sketch shows the "Interior of a Slave Shanty, near Petersburg." (fl)

two slaves and rented a third to join the booming tobacco agriculture business. In 1860, he grew 1,100 pounds on his 150 improved acres.

During the Confederate winter encampment Margaret Banks frequently opened her home to board officer's wives. An artillery captain described their hostess as "thoroughly alive to everything in the present." Her rough native accent thrilled her visitors: "She knows too a thousand old world things so that tis a treat to hear her homely talk seasoned with strong Scotch shrewdness." The widow prepared a sumptuous feast at her house on Christmas, complete with eggnog and cake. "I ate so much sponge cake that whenever you would touch me, it would be just like squeezing an India rubber ball," claimed a guest.

John joined Company B of Archer's 3rd Battalion Virginia Reserves, but little information is available regarding his service. He likely walked home after the fall of Petersburg rather than joining Lee's army on the retreat to Appomattox.

Unfortunately, the area around Lee's headquarters has been entirely transformed by modern development. The final Confederate positions stood along the eastern bank of Rohoic Creek at the border between Dinwiddie County and the city of Petersburg.

The VI Corps suffered 1,081 of the Union army's 3,936 casualties on April 2 to guarantee Petersburg's fall. Between 5,000 and 5,500 Confederates were casualties, most of the number being those captured. (loc)

The Fall of Petersburg

CHAPTER FOURTEEN

General Lee withdrew his headquarters from Edge Hill and reestablished it at Cottage Farm on the city's western outskirts. Faced with the inevitability of Petersburg's fall, he looked for a way to safely consolidate his army from its wide front. Only one escape route remained open—the Richmond & Danville Railroad—and the Confederate commander instructed for all units to move on that line. The gray chieftain selected Amelia Court House, 40 miles west of Petersburg, as the rendezvous point.

Despite the desires of President Davis to desperately hang on to the Confederate capital, Lee realized the need to immediately evacuate his army to stand a chance at a merger with Johnston's forces in North Carolina. "It is absolutely necessary that we should abandon our position tonight, or run the risk of being cut off in the morning," he wired the Secretary of War. "I have given all the orders to officers on both sides of the river, and have taken every precaution that I can to make the movement successful. It will be a difficult operation, but I hope not impracticable."

Lee's orders called for Longstreet's men and those of the Third Corps who fell back into Petersburg to cross the Battersea pontoon bridge to the north side of the Appomattox River while Gordon's corps crossed the Pocahontas and railroad bridges. Meanwhile, Lt. Gen. Richard S. Ewell, commanding the troops around Richmond, would cross the James River and march for the Genito road.

Amelia Court House lay back on the south side of the Appomattox River, so Lee issued marching orders through the tangled Chesterfield County roadways for

"This has been a hard day on us but we have been successful in all we undertook." (ea)

"As we passed through Petersburg the sidewalks were filled with weeping women and children, lamenting the fate which they knew daylight would bring them." (hw)

Ewell to cross at Genito Bridge, Mahone's Division to cross at Goode's Bridge, and the remainder to narrowly file across Bevill's Bridge. He ordered the movement for 8 p.m., with the artillery withdrawing first. He kept the pickets at their posts until 3 a.m. on April 3.

"As we passed through Petersburg the sidewalks of the city were filled with weeping women and children, lamenting the fate which they knew daylight would bring upon them," dramatized a melancholy survivor from Lane's Brigade. "In our army they had centred their hopes, and with our departure they well knew their last earthly refuge and hope were gone, and for many days and nights thereafter the wailings and lamentations of these helpless women and children rang in the Southern soldier's ear."

As they abandoned the city, Confederate officials destroyed military stores and tobacco warehouses before burning the bridges over the Appomattox, leaving Petersburg's citizens to their own fate.

Union soldiers rapidly descended into Petersburg from all directions, glad to receive "a free entrance to a place that for nine and a half months was tabooed to us by cannon & musketry." (hw)

* * *

The morning of April 3 broke clear and fair with a mild temperature. "The land was a flush of early roses," remembered a Petersburg resident. "Nature seemed as if in mockery to our woe, to have put on her loveliest dress to meet the conquering foe. . . . It was with heavy hearts and grave foreboding that we looked out on the beautiful day, and sighed and wept with a vain regret as we thought of our brave boys in gray to whom we had said farewell at midnight."

Unsure about the strength of Petersburg's inner defenses, General Wright ordered a bombardment to begin at 5 a.m. "The command will be held in readiness to assault the enemy's works in case he should be found to be evacuating or show signs of weakness," he wired, though the bombardment never commenced. Union soldiers heard noisy explosions from within the city during the night and witnessed as flames engulfed its industrial district.

"The sky was illuminated by repeated explosions

"It was yet dark when we made our way into the Court House and up the winding stairs into the clock tower." (loc)

and fires, which made it very evident that Lee was preparing to evacuate or had done so," remembered a Vermont lieutenant who longed to enter the city. "It was not light enough for us to see then so had to wait until daylight." Many units around Petersburg pressed their pickets toward its outskirts, jockeying for position to be the first to enter the Cockade City.

At 3:00 a.m., Brig. Gen. John F. Hartranft ordered the skirmishers of his Third Division of the IX Corps to "feel for the enemy" and prepared his men south of Petersburg to move on the city. Ten minutes later, Lt. Col. Ralph Ely ordered two of his Michigan regiments in the First Division of the IX Corps, stationed due east of the city, to advance along the City Point Road toward the Confederate earthworks. At 3:20 a.m., Col. Oliver Edwards instructed his brigade of the VI Corps to approach the city from the west.

The 1st Michigan Sharpshooters punched their flag through the clock tower while the 2nd Michigan planted theirs on the nearby customs house. (hw)

The race to enter Petersburg was on.

Michigan Sergeant William T. Wixcey hoped to be the first to enter town and darted ahead with his color guard. "Our way was lighted by the glare from burning tobacco warehouses," he recalled. They found everything quiet on the streets, but for a few black residents who "expressed their joy at seeing Old Glory in the hands of Marse Lincoln's soldiers" finally entering the city.

In front of the courthouse, they met a city delegate who wished to discuss a peaceful surrender.

Abraham Lincoln was accompanied at the Wallace House by his sons Tad and Robert. "He dismounted in the street, and came in through the front gate with long and rapid strides, his face beaming with delight. He seized General Grant's hand . . . and stood shaking it for some time, and pouring out his thanks and congratulations with all the fervor of a heart which seemed overflowing with its fullness of joy." (php)

The Michiganders declared they had more important business on hand and rushed into the building and wound their way up its stairs into the clock tower. "For want of a better place to display our colors we opened the door of the clock face and thrust them out thought it," remembered Wixson, "and there, for the first time in years, floated the dear old flag." At the moment, the clock displayed 4:28.

Meanwhile, Mayor William W. Townes proceeded with a delegation to the western outskirts of the city where they also hoped to find a Union officer to accept terms of Petersburg's surrender. Evidently, the VI Corps expected to find at least a token force still holding the inner defenses. As the Petersburg party reached the abandoned line, they heard a signal gun fire near Fort Gregg. "Instantaneously there sprang forth, as from the bowels of the earth . . . a mighty host of Federal soldiers, and then followed such a shout of victory as seemed to shake the very ground on which we stood."

A New York officer explained the commotion: "Just as day was dawning I was ordered to advance my line toward the town quickly, which I did, charging at double-quick, and did not halt until my men were in the streets of Petersburg." Eventually, city officials worked out an agreement to protect Petersburg's property and inhabitants.

Additional Union soldiers poured into the conquered city, eager to view their long-awaited prize. Later in the morning, Grant established his headquarters at the Wallace house on Market Street. Soon, Meade rode into town to discuss the city's occupation and pursuit of Lee. As Col. Theodore Lyman passed through the outskirts with Meade, he found them to be "very poor" but enjoyed seeing the broad grins of the black families that greeted him. Meanwhile Petersburg's white residents glared "from broken windows with an air of lazy dislike."

Captain Darius J. Safford of the 1st Vermont Heavy Artillery was taken prisoner the previous June at the battle of the Weldon Railroad and had spent a few days captive in town before making his escape. The captain was happy to make his return: "I went into the town and saw the place of my confinement, where I slept the first night, where I was marched through the streets of the then defiant city, now humbled before the power they so hated and despised."

Safford recalled the enthusiastic reaction of the large free black and enslaved population. He especially recalled "their great delight in seeing the colored troops marching through the city."

As more VI Corps soldiers filed into town, they heard loud cheers ring the air from the right of their column. Rhode Islander George B. Peck looked in that direction and spotted President Lincoln riding into town around

10:30 a.m. "With hat in hand he graciously acknowledged the greetings of the soldiers, who enthusiastically swung their caps high in air, and made the city ring with their loud hurrahs," he recalled. "His careworn countenance was illumed with a benignant smile; it was the hour of triumph; he was receiving the reward of four years of unparalleled toil, anxiety and care."

The president arrived at the Wallace house by 11 a.m. to meet with Grant. He jokingly congratulated the Union commander on his success: "Do you know, general, that I have had a sort of a sneaking idea for some days that you intended to do something like this." The two discussed the likely surrender of the Confederate army for an hour and a half and eagerly awaited news from Richmond before Lincoln saddled up once more and returned to City Point.

Shortly after Lincoln's departure, Grant received cheering news from Maj. Gen. Godfrey Weitzel, commanding the XXV Corps. Weitzel wrote that he had taken possession of an abandoned Richmond at 8:15 that morning. Satisfied with the update, Grant left Petersburg to join his army already in pursuit of Lee's retreat.

Like in Petersburg, Confederate officials in Richmond set fire to many items of military, political, and economic importance in advance of the triumphant Union army's arrival into the capital. (fl)

*   *   *

Six days later, General Grant would meet with the Confederate commander 80 miles to the west at Appomattox Court House to discuss the surrender of the Army of Northern Virginia. For the next 150 years, historians have contemplated various "what-if" scenarios for that one-week stretch between April 2-9, when various misfortunes compounded Lee's attempt to flee his pursuers and continue the war indefinitely.

The reality is that the decisive Union breakthrough on the morning of April 2 firmly placed Grant in the driver's seat for the final campaign. The Union army carried through their control of the military initiative Grant aggressively sought 11 months previously and finally brought an end to the tragic conflict that gripped the nation for four years.

Perhaps a Vermont private was not far off on the evening of April 2, 1865, when he wrote his father: "This has been one of the greatest days in American History."

Field Fortifications:
A Glossary of Terms
APPENDIX A

The 292-day campaign around Petersburg is most often associated with the sprawling fortifications that dominated the region. The proper terms for the particular arrangement of sticks and dirt that transformed the landscape into perfect killing fields can prove baffling. To aid in understanding these terms, they are arranged in the order that an attacking army would encounter them.

VIDETTE—The most advanced sentry, usually mounted.

RIFLE PIT—A small pit in front of the main fortification designed for just a few pickets.

ABATIS—Tangled tree limbs and branches interlaced together with their pointed ends facing the enemy.

CHEVAUX-DE-FRISE—Horizontal log with sharp wooden lances inserted at 45-degree angles to present a wooden fence. Designed for mobility to use at the beginning of earthwork construction or to remove to facilitate an attack.

PALISADE—A line of sharpened stick angled toward the attacker to stop or slow their movement.

GLACIS—Gentle slope leading up to the beginning of the ditch in front of the fortification.

COUNTERSCARP—Outer sloped wall of the ditch.

DITCH—The large deep trench made around each work.

SCARP—Inner sloped wall of the ditch.

BERM—Small horizontal space between the top of the ditch and bottom of the parapet—designed to prevent earthwork from tumbling back into its ditch.

FRAISE—Stakes or palisades placed horizontally along the berm to stop or slow a climbing attacker and to prevent the work from being taken by surprise.

RAMPART—Broad earthen embankment surrounding a fortified place.

PARAPET—The top of the rampart.

REVETMENT—Support for the embankment—oftentimes made of wood, sandbags, gabion, or masonry—to protect against erosion.

GABION—A woven cylinder of sticks made in advance to quickly build or repair the parapet.

BREASTWORK—Fortification made out of piled material—logs, fence rails, stones—usually created up to breast height. Sometimes then covered by the rampart when used long-term.

EMBRASURE—An opening or hole through the work through which the cannon are fired.

SALLY PORT—Passages leading from the inner to the outer works.

BANQUETTE—A raised step behind the parapet serving as a firing platform for defenders.

TRAVERSE—Small rampart perpendicular to the parapet to protect against flanking fire and limit a successful attacker from expanding their breech.

FORT—A fully enclosed earthwork.

Union troopers camped at Mangohick Church during the march to rejoin the Army of the Potomac. The church was used temporarily by Generals Grant and Meade as a headquarters during the Overland Campaign. (dd)

"The Hardships of This March"
Sheridan's Return to the Army of the Potomac

APPENDIX B
BY DANIEL T. DAVIS

A winter rain fell as a crisp, biting wind cut across the landscape surrounding Winchester, Virginia. Withstanding the cold and the snow on the ground, the troopers readied themselves for a long march. Their commander, Maj. Gen. Philip H. Sheridan, was preparing for a movement south up the Shenandoah Valley. Sheridan had been in the Valley since August 1864. He had been dispatched there by general in chief Lt. Gen. Ulysses S. Grant to deal with the Rebel threat in the region posed by Lt. Gen. Jubal Early's Army of the Valley. In a little more than a month, between September and October, Sheridan defeated Early in a succession of battles at Third Winchester, Fisher's Hill, and Tom's Brook. His crowning victory came on October 19 along the banks of a stream called Cedar Creek. There, "Little Phil" as he was known, smashed Robert E. Lee's "Bad Old Man" and effectively put to rest any prospects of future Confederate operations in the Valley.

With the campaign ending and the advent of winter arriving, Sheridan's units began to leave the Valley, bound for service elsewhere. The VI Corps set out for a return back to the siege lines around Richmond and Petersburg in late November 1864 while elements of the XIX Corps were sent to Savannah, Georgia. Sheridan's VIII Corps—the Army of West Virginia—joined their comrades at Petersburg, while still others were sent to West Virginia. By late December, the Army of the Shenandoah was a mere shell of its former self. Under the overall leadership of Brig. Gen. Wesley Merritt, Sheridan's force consisted of Brig. Gen. Thomas Devin's First Cavalry Division and Bvt. Maj. Gen. George Armstrong Custer's Third Cavalry Division.

Under orders from Grant, Sheridan was to wreck the Virginia Central Railroad and the James River Canal before moving on to Lynchburg, Virginia. From there, Sheridan was given the choice of returning to Winchester or continuing into North Carolina to join up with Maj. Gen. William Tecumseh Sherman's army group.

Little Phil wrote after the war that his force consisted of "10,000 officers and men . . . eight ambulances, sixteen ammunition wagons, a pontoon train for eight canvas boats, and a small supply train." Rightly deemed a grand spectacle by one local resident, Sheridan set out from Winchester on February 27, 1865. Passing all-

George Armstrong Custer showed tremendous battlefield instincts and an eye for the terrain that eventually failed him after the war at Little Big Horn. (loc)

Jubal Anderson Early refused to surrender at the end of the war and fled to Mexico before moving to Canada where he wrote his memoirs that helped establish the "Lost Cause" narrative of the war. (loc)

too-familiar places, the troopers rode along "at a steady gait," reaching the village of Woodstock on the first day. The following day's march was not as pleasant: the troopers had to cross the rain-swollen North Fork of the Shenandoah River. In a harrowing ordeal, eight men drowned as they attempted to cross.

On the fourth day of the ride, the cavalry reached Staunton and the site of Jubal Early's winter encampment. The Rebels, however, were nowhere to be seen. Old Jube had taken what was left of his force and moved east toward Waynesboro and out of his enemy's line of march. The tiny village lay along the Virginia Central, one of Sheridan's strategic objectives. Ever the aggressor, Sheridan decided to give chase. With Custer's division leading the advance, Sheridan rode out in pursuit of his old foe.

He remembered that the "by-roads were miry beyond description, rain having fallen almost incessantly since we left Winchester, but notwithstanding the downpour the column pushed on, men and horses growing almost unrecognizable from the mud covering them from head to foot."

On the afternoon of March 2, Custer's skirmishers reached Waynesboro. Before them stood their familiar Rebel adversary. Early's line ran from north of the village to a point below it near the South River. Unfortunately, the lack of manpower did not allow him to extend all the way to the riverbank, leaving a dangerous gap on his left flank. This mistake did not go unnoticed by Custer.

Deciding on a battle plan similar to the one he had employed months earlier at Tom's Brook, Custer decided to pin the Confederates in place while he sent a force around their flank. As Col. William Wells's brigade moved forward to probe the enemy position, Custer dispatched the 1st Connecticut, 2nd Ohio, and 3rd New Jersey around to his right and toward the opening between the Rebel left and the river. Moving ahead dismounted, these three regiments rushed into the opening and quickly threatened to trap the Confederates in a pincer. Early's line collapsed as his frightened soldiers scrambled to safety. In all, Custer's division captured more than 1,200 Confederates along with 11 cannons.

Following his triumph at Waynesboro, Sheridan resumed the march the next day toward Charlottesville. Reaching its outskirts, Custer was met by a deputation of citizens, led by the mayor, who summarily surrendered the town.

From Charlottesville, Sheridan decided to "move toward . . . Amherst Court House . . . so Devin, under Merritt's supervision marched along the James River, destroying the canal while Custer pushed ahead on the railroad and broke it up." Little Phil anticipated that the two columns would unite around New Market, cross the James, and then head south into North Carolina to find Sherman. Not surprisingly the James was flooded due to the early spring rains. This impassable route left Sheridan to cast about for other options.

He had long since decided against returning to Winchester, having told his officers such on the morning of the second day. He was, however, much closer to Grant than to Sherman's force. Accordingly, Little Phil concluded that he would "destroy still more thoroughly the James River canal and the Virginia Central railroad and then join General Grant in front of Petersburg."

Sheridan headed his columns east on the morning of March 9. Anticipating that his men would need provisions, he sent a courier through to Grant to have supplies sent to White House Landing on the Pamunkey River. For nine days, the Union troopers rampaged across the Virginia countryside. Along with wrecking the canal and the railroad, they destroyed 1,000 bushels of wheat and 500 bushels of salt.

Sheridan's control of the Shenandoah Valley forced the Confederates in Petersburg to be even more reliant on their tenuous rail connections to the south. (hw)

On March 18, Sheridan reached White House Landing. To his "relief," the requested supplies were waiting for them.

After the war, Sheridan would write that "the hardships of this march far exceeded those of any previous campaigns by the cavalry. Almost incessant rains had drenched us for sixteen days and nights, and the swollen streams and wellnigh bottomless roads . . . presented grave difficulties on every hand, but surmounting them all, we destroyed the enemy's means of subsistence . . . and permanently crippled the Virginia Central railroad, as well as the James River canal." He added that his men's spirits were "buoyed up by the cheering thought that we should soon take part in the final struggle of the war."

Sheridan's troopers received a welcome respite at White House Landing, remaining there for the next week. On March 25, they set out on the final leg of their journey to Petersburg, reaching the Union lines two days later. Sheridan had left victory behind in the Shenandoah Valley. Now, the impetuous commander hoped to garner additional laurels around Petersburg.

Grant put him to work immediately.

DANIEL T. DAVIS, the managing editor of Emerging Civil War, is the co-author of Bloody Autumn: The Shenandoah Valley Campaign of 1864, Hurricane from the Heavens: The Battle of Cold Harbor, and Calamity in Carolina: The Battles of Averasboro and Bentonville.

Pamplin Historical Park preserves many of the sites associated with the final battles for Petersburg, including the Breakthrough site. (rm)

Pamplin Historical Park

APPENDIX C

BY EDWARD S. ALEXANDER

The remarkably impressive earthworks stormed by the Union VI Corps still stand today due to a mixture of luck and family devotion for more than 130 years. In many areas around Petersburg, the large swaths of the earthworks were immediately restored back into farmland after the war, but a significant chunk of Wilcox's line remained untouched. When the National Park Service established the boundaries of Petersburg National Battlefield, however, the site of the Breakthrough still remained unprotected.

Finally in the early 1990s, when the landowners were looking to sell the property, the Association for the Preservation of Civil War Sites (today the Civil War Trust) turned to Dr. Robert Boisseau Pamplin, Jr., for assistance in preserving these remarkable earthworks. An accomplished businessman and generous philanthropist, Bob Pamplin had a special association to the land.

The Boisseau family arrived in America in the late 1600s seeking freedom from religious persecution in their native France. By the middle of the next century, the family was settled into Dinwiddie County, Virginia. Around 1812, William Boisseau began construction of Tudor Hall along Arthur's Swamp for his growing family. He had married Athaliah Keziah Wright Goodwyn in 1808, and the pair had seven children survive to maturity.

A prominent tobacco inspector in Petersburg, William's farm was also growing into a thriving tobacco plantation, nearly reaching a thousand acres by his death in 1838. The bulk of the labor, however, fell on the backs of the 51 slaves William owned upon his death.

As was common upon the death of a patriarch, the plantation's land and slaves were divided among William's children. Athaliah, however, assumed management of Tudor Hall. In the late 1840s, her son Joseph Goodwyn Boisseau took over the property and spent the next decade expanding and renovating the house for his own family's use. Tragically none of Joseph and his wife Ann Jane Clarke's three children survived past their eighth birthday.

It is through Joseph's niece Ella—who spent significant time at Tudor Hall with her grandmother, Athaliah—that the Pamplin family is connected with the property.

Trenches near the Breakthrough (ea)

Ella's daughter Pauline married John Robert Pamplin in 1898.

Joseph, meanwhile, spent the 1850s surveying roads in northern Dinwiddie County and adopting his agricultural practice to reflect a smaller acreage of land and inherited slaves than his father had owned. The 1860 census shows that Joseph's property included 219 acres of land—only 119 under cultivation—and 18 slaves. While the rest of the county boomed with tobacco agriculture in the decade before the war, Joseph contented himself with a market farm reflective of his property. He raised livestock and grew wheat, corn, oats, and potatoes.

While the outbreak war ravaged farms and families across Virginia for its first three years, Dinwiddie County remained largely unaffected outside of the military scope. That all changed in the autumn of 1864 when Ulysses S. Grant began targeting the supply routes through the county that fed into Petersburg and Richmond. Upon the arrival of both armies to the area during the September-October fighting around Peebles Farm, Joseph and Ann left Tudor Hall to stay with family. Brigadier General Samuel McGowan took over their vacated home as his headquarters, and his 1,400 South Carolinians encamped in the surrounding fields.

Over the winter, the Confederate soldiers cut down the forests and constructed their elaborate, protective fortifications. By spring, the ground prepared for the

Earthworks at the Hart Farm
(ea)

anticipated Union assault but were ordered down to Hatcher's Run at the end of March and the lines inherited by James H. Lane's North Carolinians.

The Vermont Brigade's initial breakthrough took place just a short distance from Tudor Hall. A tradition states that the home was used as a hospital after the battle, but no evidence backs up the claim.

The ultimate Union victory meant freedom for the slaves at Tudor Hall and forced yet another change in the property's business model. When Joseph Boisseau returned after the war, he found his family's land devastated by the conflict. Nearly 50 years old, and with no surviving children of his own, Joseph left the barren land mostly alone and let forests grow back in his former fields.

Four years after the war, he sold his property to Asahel H. Gerow from New York and moved into Petersburg with Ann. The Gerow family decided against revitalizing the land as a large-scale farm. Asahel's son, Smith T. Gerow, saw the value in commercial timbering and made special provisions for the operations not to affect the earthworks. This delicate arrangement remained through the 20th century until the land's pending sale, when the APCWS looked to Boisseau descendants for help.

Bob Pamplin surprised the APCWS with a generous offer to not only purchase the land to preserve the earthworks, but to build an interpretive park to deliver its educational message. Over time, this original 100-acre

Trail construction at Pamplin
(php)

park has blossomed into "the new crown jewel of Civil War history destinations in America."

The National Museum of the Civil War Soldier tells the joint story of the Northern and Southern soldiers using interactive audio technology. Rather than focusing on tactics or generalship, the premier exhibit "Duty Called Me Here: The Common Soldier's Experience in the American Civil War" focuses on the transformative experience from civilian into soldier.

Tudor Hall has been restored to its wartime appearance, and many of the plantation's outbuildings have been reconstructed to bring light to the story of the region's slaves, whose unique experiences were often intentionally avoided in past decades of Civil War remembrance.

Civil War Adventure Camp (ea)

The park has also historically restored the exterior of two more antebellum homes. The grounds of the Banks house, which served as Ulysses S. Grant's headquarters on April 2, is accessible with park admission. A short walk from the Battlefield Center will bring a visitor the Hart house where Seymour's division crashed through the Confederate lines during the Breakthrough.

The campus of the Civil War Adventure Camp is visible from the back porch of the Hart house. This immersion experience offers visitors the unique opportunity to enlist for an 18-hour period as a Civil War soldier. Once equipped for the army, they drill, march, eat, and bunk as soldiers and participate in tactical engagements before actually firing a rifle, cannon, and mortar.

National Museum of the Civil War Soldier (php)

The Fortifications Exhibit provides a stunning visual display of how the earthworks would have looked during the war, and the Battlefield Center offers an overall strategic picture of the Petersburg campaign and what led the armies to the final decisive struggle just a stone's throw from the museum's door.

**Pamplin Historical Park
GPS: N 37.18289 W 77.47992**

The Breakthrough Trail leads visitors on a journey that can run from a third of a mile to nearly five miles to walk in the footsteps of the soldiers who forever marked this land as hallowed ground.

THE BATTLES FOR PETERSBURG
MARCH-APRIL 1865

Because of the size of the front and the constant shifting of troops from point to point, the Order of Battle focuses on those units engaged in the breakthrough rather than the entire armies.

The Union Army
Lt. Gen. Ulysses S. Grant

ARMY OF THE POTOMAC
Maj. Gen. George G. Meade

SECOND CORPS Maj. Gen. Andrew A. Humphreys
FIRST DIVISION Brig. Gen. Nelson A. Miles
First Brigade Col. George W. Scott
Second Brigade Col. Robert Nugent
Third Brigade Col. Henry J. Madill
Fourth Brigade Col. John Ramsey

SECOND DIVISION Brig. Gen. William Hays
First Brigade Col. William Olmstead
Second Brigade Col. James P. McIvor
Third Brigade Brig. Gen. Thomas A. Smyth

THIRD DIVISION Brig. Gen. Gershom Mott
First Brigade Brig. Gen. Regis de Trobriand
Second Brigade Brig. Gen. Byron R. Pierce
Third Brigade Col. Robert McAllister

ARTILLERY Maj. John G. Hazard

FIFTH CORPS Maj. Gen. Gouverneur K. Warren
FIRST DIVISION Brig. Gen. Charles Griffin
First Brigade Brig. Gen. Joshua L, Chamberlain
Second Brigade Col. Edward M. Gregory
Third Brigade Brig. Gen. Joseph J. Bartlett

SECOND DIVISION Brig. Gen. Romeyn B. Ayres
First Brigade Col. Frederick Winthrop[1], Col. James G. Grindlay
Second Brigade Brig. Gen. Andrew W. Dension[2], Col. Richard N. Bowerman[3], Col. David L. Stanton
Third Brigade Col. James Gwyn

THIRD DIVISION Brig. Gen. Samuel W. Crawford
First Brigade Col. John A. Kellogg
Second Brigade Brig. Gen. Henry Baxter
Third Brigade Col. Richard Coulter

ARTILLERY Col. Charles S. Wainwright

SIXTH CORPS Maj. Horatio Gouverneur Wright
FIRST DIVISION Brig. Gen. Frank Wheaton
First Brigade Col. William Henry Penrose
*1st & 4th New Jersey · 2nd New Jersey · 3rd New Jersey · 10th New Jersey · 15th New Jersey
40th New Jersey*

Second Brigade Col. Joseph Eldridge Hamblin
2nd Connecticut Heavy Artillery · 65th New York · 121st New York · 95th Pennsylvania

Third Brigade Col. Oliver Edwards
*37th Massachusetts · 49th Pennsylvania · 82nd Pennsylvania · 119th Pennsylvania · 2nd Rhode Island
5th Wisconsin*

SECOND DIVISION Brig. Gen. George Washington Getty
First Brigade Col. James Meech Warner
62nd New York · 93rd Pennsylvania · 98th Pennsylvania · 102nd Pennsylvania · 139th Pennsylvania

Second Brigade Brig. Gen. Lewis Addison Grant[4]
1st Vermont Heavy Artillery · 2nd Vermont · 3rd Vermont · 4th Vermont · 5th Vermont · 6th Vermont

Third Brigade Col. Thomas Worcester Hyde
1st Maine Veteran · 43rd New York · 49th New York · 77th New York · 122nd New York · 61st Pennsylvania

THIRD DIVISION Brig. Gen. Truman Seymour
First Brigade Col. William Snyder Truex
14th New Jersey · 106th New York · 151st New York · 87th Pennsylvania · 10th Vermont

Second Brigade Col. Joseph Warren Keifer
*6th Maryland · 9th New York Heavy Artillery · 110th Ohio · 122nd Ohio · 126th Ohio
67th Pennsylvania · 138th Pennsylvania*

ARTILLERY Capt. Andrew Cowan
*1st New Jersey, Battery A · 1st New York · 3rd New York · 1st Rhode Island, Battery G
1st Rhode Island, Battery H · 5th United States, Battery E · 3rd Vermont*

NINTH CORPS Maj. Gen. John G. Parke
FIRST DIVISION Brig. Gen. Orlando B. Willcox
First Brigade Col. Samuel Harriman
Second Brigade Lt. Col. Ralph Ely
Third Brigade Lt. Col. Gilbert Robinson

SECOND DIVISION Brig. Gen. Robert B. Potter
First Brigade Col. John I. Curtin
Second Brigade Brig. Gen. Simon G. Griffin

THIRD DIVISION Brig. Gen. John F. Hartranft
First Brigade Lt. Col. H.H. McCall
Second Brigade Col. Joseph A. Mathews

Independent Brigade Col. Charles H.T. Collis

ARTILLERY Col. John C. Tidball

CAVARLY Maj. Gen. Philip H. Sheridan
Army of the Shenandoah Brig. Gen. Wesley Merritt
FIRST DIVISION Brig. Gen. Thomas C. Devin
First Brigade Col. Peter Stagg
Second Brigade Col. Charles L. Fitzhugh
Third Brigade Brig. Gen. Alfred Gibbs

THIRD DIVISION Brig. Gen. George A. Custer
First Brigade Col. Alexander C.M. Pennington
Second Brigade Col. William Wells
Third Brigade Col. Henry Capehart

SECOND DIVISION *(Army of the Potomac)* Maj. Gen. George Crook
First Brigade Brig. Gen. Henry E. Davies
Second Brigade Col. J. Irvin Gregg
Third Brigade Col. Charles H. Smith

ARMY OF THE JAMES
Maj. Gen. Edward O. C. Ord

Defenses of Bermuda Hundred Maj. Gen. George L. Hartsuff

INFANTRY DIVISION Maj. Gen. Edward Ferrero
First Brigade Col. Gilbert H. McKibbin
Second Brigade Col. George C. Kibbe

Separate Brigade Brig. Gen. Joseph B. Carr
Fort Pocahontas Lt. Col. Ashbel W. Angel
Harrison's Landing Col. Wardwell G. Robinson
Fort Powhatan Col. William J. Sewell

ARTILLERY Col. Henry L. Abbott

TWENTY-FOURTH CORPS Maj. Gen. John Gibbon
FIRST DIVISION Brig. Gen. Robert S. Foster
First Brigade Col. Thomas O. Osborn
Third Brigade Col. George B. Dandy
Fourth Brigade Col. Harrison S. Fairchild

THIRD DIVISION Brig. Gen. Charles Devens
First Brigade Col. Edward H. Ripley
Second Brigade Col. Michael T. Donohoe
Third Brigade Col. Samuel H. Roberts

INDEPENDENT DIVISION Brig. Gen. John W. Turner
First Brigade Lt. Col. Andrew Potter
Second Brigade Col. William B. Curtis
Third Brigade Brig. Gen. Thomas M. Harris

ARTILLERY Maj. Charles C. Abell

TWENTY-FIFTH CORPS Maj. Gen. Godfrey Weitzel
FIRST DIVISION Brig. Gen. August V. Kautz
First Brigade Col. Alonzo G. Draper
Second Brigade Brig. Gen. Edward A. Wild
Third Brigade Brig. Gen. Henry G. Thomas
Attached Brigade Col. Charles S. Russell

SECOND DIVISION Brig. Gen. William Birney
First Brigade Col. James Shaw Jr.
Second Brigade Col. Ulysses Doubleday
Third Brigade Col. William W. Woodward

Artillery Capt. Loomis L. Langdon

CAVALRY DIVISION Brig. Gen. Ranald S. Mackenzie
First Brigade Col. Robert M. West
Second Brigade Col. Samuel P. Spear

1 mortally wounded April 1
2 wounded March 31
3 wounded April 1
4 wounded April 2

ARMY OF NORTHERN VIRGINIA
Gen. Robert E. Lee

FIRST CORPS Lt. Gen. James Longstreet
PICKETT'S DIVISION Maj. Gen. George E. Pickett
Steuart's Brigade Brig. Gen. George E. Steuart
Corse's Brigade Brig. Gen. Montgomeroy Corse
Hunton's Brigade Brig. Gen. Eppa Hunton
Terry's Brigade Brig. Gen. William R. Terry[1], Maj. William W. Bentley

FIELD'S DIVISION Maj. Gen. Charles W. Field
Perry's Brigade Brig. Gen. William F. Perry
Anderson's Brigade Brig. Gen. George T. Anderson
Benning's Brigade Brig. Gen. Henry L. Benning
Gregg's Brigade Col. Robert M. Powell
Bratton's Brigade Brig. Gen. John Bratton

KERSHAW'S DIVISION Maj. Gen. Joseph B. Kershaw
DuBose's Brigade Brig. Gen. Dudley M. DuBose
Humphrey's Brigade Col. William H. Fitzgerald
Simms's Brigade Brig. Gen. James P. Simms

ARTILLERY Brig. Gen. Edward P. Alexander
Cabell's Battalion Col. Henry C. Cabell
Hardaway's Battalion Lt. Col. Richard A. Hardaway
Haskell's Battalion Maj. John C. Haskell
Huger's Battalion Maj. Tyler C. Jordan
Johnson's Battalion Maj. Marmaduke Johnson
Stark's Battalion Lt. Col. Alexander W. Stark

SECOND CORPS Maj. Gen. John B. Gordon
GRIMES'S DIVISION Maj. Gen. Bryan Grimes
Battle's Brigade Col. Edwin L. Hobson
Grimes's Brigade Col. David G. Cowand
Cox's Brigade Brig. Gen. William R. Cox
Cook's Brigade Col. Edwin A. Nash
Archer's Battalion Lt. Col. Fletcher H. Archer

EARLY'S DIVISION Brig. Gen. James A. Walker
Johnston's Brigade Col. John W. Lea
Lewis's Brigade Capt. John Beard
Walker's Brigade Maj. Henry Kyd Douglas

GORDON'S DIVISION Brig. Gen. Clement A. Evans
Evans's Brigade Col. John H. Lowe
Terry's Brigade Col. Titus V. Williams
York's Brigade Col. Eugene Waggaman

ARTILLERY Brig. Gen. Armistead Long
Braxton's Battalion Lt. Col. Carter M. Braxton
Cutshaw's Battalion Maj. Wilfred E. Cutshaw
Nelson's Battalion Lt. Col. William Nelson

THIRD CORPS Lt. Gen. Ambrose Powell Hill[2]
HETH'S DIVISION Maj. Gen. Henry Heth
Davis' Brigade Brig. Gen. Joseph Robert Davis, Col. Andrew McCampbell Nelson[3]
1st Confederate Battalion · 2nd Mississippi · 11th Mississippi · 26th Mississippi · 42nd Mississippi

Cooke's Brigade Brig. Gen. John Rogers Cooke
15th North Carolina · 27th North Carolina · 46th North Carolina · 48th North Carolina · 55th North Carolina

MacRae's Brigade Brig. Gen. William MacRae
*11th North Carolina · 26th North Carolina · 44th North Carolina · 47th North Carolina
52nd North Carolina*

McComb's Brigade Brig. Gen. William McComb
*2nd Maryland Battalion · 1st Tennessee Provisional · 7th Tennessee · 14th Tennessee
17th & 23rd Tennessee · 25th & 44th Tennessee · 63rd Tennessee*

WILCOX'S DIVISION Maj. Gen. Cadmus Marcellus Wilcox
Thomas's Brigade Brig. Gen. Edward Lloyd Thomas
14th Georgia · 35th Georgia · 45th Georgia · 49th Georgia

Lane's Brigade Brig. Gen. James Henry Lane
18th North Carolina · 28th North Carolina · 33rd North Carolina · 37th North Carolina

McGowan's Brigade Brig. Gen. Samuel McGowan
*1st South Carolina Provisional · 12th South Carolina · 13th South Carolina · 14th South Carolina
Orr's Rifles*

Scales's Brigade Col. Joseph Henry Hyman
13th North Carolina · 16th North Carolina · 22nd North Carolina · 34th North Carolina · 38th North Carolina

MAHONE'S DIVISION Maj. Gen. William Mahone
Forney's Brigade Brig. Gen. William H. Forney
Weisiger Brigade Brig. Gen. David A. Weisiger
Harris's Brigade Brig. Gen. Nathaniel H. Harris
Sorrel's Brigade Col. George E. Taylor
Finegan's Brigade Col. David Lang

ARTILLERY Brig. Gen. Reuben Lindsay Walker
McIntosh's Battalion Col. David G. McIntosh
Pegram's Battalion Col. William J. Pegram[4], Maj. Joseph McGraw
Poague's Battalion Lt. Col. William T. Poague
Richardson's Battery Maj. Victor Maurin
Cutts's Battalion Lt. Col. John Lane
Eshleman's Battalion Lt. Col. Benjamin F. Eshleman
Owen's Battalion Lt. Col. William M. Owen

ANDERSON'S CORPS Lt. Gen. Richard H. Anderson
JOHNSON'S DIVISION Maj. Gen. Bushrod R. Johnson
Wise's Brigade Brig. Gen. Henry A. Wise
Wallace's Brigade Brig. Gen. William H. Wallace
Moody's Brigade Brig. Gen. Young M. Moody
Ransom's Brigade Brig. Gen. Matthew W. Ransom

ARTILLERY Col. Hilary P. Jones
Moseley's Battalion Maj. William H. Caskie
Branch's Battalion Maj. James C. Coit
Stribling's Battalion Maj. Joseph G. Blount

CAVALRY CORPS Maj. Gen. Fitzhugh Lee
FITZHUGH LEE'S DIVISION Brig. Gen. Thomas T. Munford
Payne's Brigade Brig. Gen. William H. Payne[5], Col. Reuben B. Boston
Munford's Brigade
Gary's Brigade Brig. Gen. Martin W. Gary

W. H. F. LEE'S DIVISION Maj. Gen. William H.F. "Rooney" Lee
Barringer's Brigade Brig. Gen. Rufus Barringer
Beale's Brigade Capt. Samuel H. Burt
Roberts's Brigade Brig. Gen. William P. Roberts

ROSSER'S DIVISION Maj. Gen. Thomas L. Rosser
Dearing's Brigade Brig. Gen. James Dearing
McCausland's Brigade

ARTILLERY Lt. Col. R. Preston Chew
Breathed's Battalion Maj. James Breathed
Chew's Battalion

1 wounded March 31
2 killed April 2
3 in command April 2
4 killed April 1
5 wounded March 30

$\mathcal{S}$uggested $\mathcal{R}$eading
THE BATTLES FOR PETERSBURG
MARCH-APRIL 1865

The Petersburg Campaign, Volume II: The Western Front Battles, September 1864-April 1865
Edwin C. Bearss
Savas Beatie (2014)
ISBN-13: 978-1-61121-104-7

Based on manuscripts prepared in the 1960s to support troop movement maps, this collection of battle narratives provides a clear overhead picture of the complicated tactics in the second half of offensives against Petersburg and its supply lines.

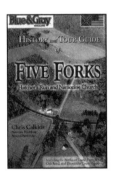

History and Tour Guide of Five Forks, Hatcher's Run and Namozine Church
Chris Calkins
Blue & Gray Enterprises (2003)
ISBN-13: 978-1-89151-507-1

This reader-friendly guide from the producers of *Blue & Gray* magazine covers the engagements leading up to and after the Breakthrough.

*The Confederate Alamo: Bloodbath at Petersburg's
Fort Gregg on April 2, 1865*
John J. Fox, III
Angle Valley Press (2010)
ISBN-13: 978-0-97119-500-4

This is one of the best micro-tactical books on a particular subject. In addition to a masterful telling of the frenzied struggle on the ramparts of Fort Gregg, the author offers many modern insights and questions about the battle's events and controversies.

Civil War Petersburg: Confederate City in the Crucible of War
A. Wilson Greene
University of Virginia Press (2006)
ISBN-13: 978-0-81392-570-7

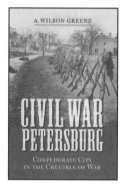

Greene offers an impressive blending of the experiences on Petersburg's home front as its residents suddenly found their city at the front lines of the war in Virginia.

*The Final Battles of the Petersburg Campaign:
Breaking the Backbone of the Rebellion*
A. Wilson Greene
The University of Tennessee Press (2008, second edition)
ISBN-13: 978-1-57233-610-0

This is the definitive "must-read" book to gain the fullest appreciation and understanding of the story featured in *Dawn of Victory*. Greene expertly follows the military action as it winds its way across Dinwiddie County while bringing its characters to remarkable life with a rich usage of personal accounts.

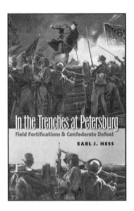

In the Trenches at Petersburg: Field Fortifications &
Confederate Defeat
Earl J. Hess
The University of North Carolina Press (2009)
ISBN-13: 978-0-8078-3282-0

The third in a trilogy on field fortifications in the Eastern
Theater of the Civil War, this book offers an impressive
study of construction and utilization of this feature that
oftentimes defined the fighting around Petersburg.

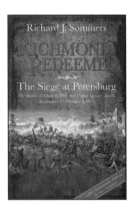

Richmond Redeemed: The Siege at Petersburg,
The Battles of Chaffin's Bluff and Poplar Spring Church,
September 29-October 2, 1864
Richard J. Sommers
Savas Beatie (2014, revised sesquicentennial edition)
ISBN-13: 978-1-61121-210-5

The updated version of Sommers's brilliant 1981
chronicling of the Fifth Offensive against Petersburg that
brought both armies to the ground now preserved by
Pamplin Historical Park.

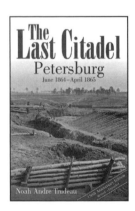

The Last Citadel: Petersburg, June 1864-April 1865
Noah Andre Trudeau
Savas Beatie (2014, revised sesquicentennial edition)
ISBN-13: 978-1-61121-212-9

This is an updated version of the single volume, from
1991, that offered the first modern take on the lengthy
struggle. Trudeau provides short but sweet narrative of
its many engagements while crafting them together to
provide the overall political, military, and social context
of the 292-day campaign.

Though the fighting upon these earthworks lasted no more than thirty minutes, its effect on the culmination of the 292-day Petersburg campaign make it one of the most decisive battles of the war. (ea)

About the Author

Edward S. Alexander is a park ranger at Pamplin Historical Park and the National Museum of the Civil War Soldier, site of the Breakthrough Battlefield in Petersburg, Virginia. His work in preserving, maintaining, and interpreting these grounds allows him to guide readers across this hallowed landscape.

Edward is a 2009 graduate of the University of Illinois with a B.A. in History and then began his career as a public historian at Fredericksburg & Spotsylvania National Military Park. He is also a contributing author at Emerging Civil War (www. emergingcivilwar.com). Edward currently resides in Richmond, Virginia.